Francis Ponge
and the
Nature of Things

Francis Ponge and the Nature of Things

From Ancient Atomism to a Modern Poetics

Patrick Meadows

Lewisburg
Bucknell University Press
London: Associated University Presses

© 1997 by Associated University Presses, Inc.

All rights reserved. Authorization to photocopy items for internal or personal use, or the internal or personal use of specific clients, is granted by the copyright owner, provided that a base fee of $10.00, plus eight cents per page, per copy is paid directly to the Copyright Clearance Center, 222 Rosewood Dr., Danvers, Massachusetts 01923. [0-8387-5360-4/97 $10.00 + 8¢ pp, pc.]

Associated University Presses
440 Forsgate Drive
Cranbury, N.J. 08512

Associated University Presses
16 Barter Street
London WC1A 2AH, England

Associated University Presses
P.O. Box 338, Port Credit
Mississauga, Ontario
Canada L5G 4L8

The paper used in this publication meets the requirements of the American National Standard for Permanence of Paper for Printed Library Materials Z39.48–1984.

Library of Congress Cataloging-in-Publication Data

Meadows, Patrick Alan.
    Francis Ponge and the nature of things : from ancient atomism to a modern poetics / Patrick Meadows.
       p. cm.
    Includes bibliographical references.
    ISBN 0-8387-5360-4 (alk. paper)
    1. Ponge, Francis—Criticism and interpretation. I. Title.
PQ2631.0643Z743   1997
841'.914—dc21   97-6998
                                                                                   CIP

PRINTED IN THE UNITED STATES OF AMERICA

Là seulement [dans les peintures de Braque], nous pouvons voir comme, dans le vide, se font et se défont les choses, comme elles naissent et meurent et renaissent autres, par la permutation de leurs éléments. Et ainsi, voyons-nous le *tout*, où rien ne se crée jamais de rien. Et pouvons-nous voir aussi les dieux, dans leurs paisibles demeures, les dieux qui ne s'occupent pas de nous et qui ne sont, pour nous, que des modèles de vie heureuse.
—Ponge, "Braque ou un méditatif à l'oeuvre"

But in them [Braque's paintings], we can see how, in the void, things are made and come undone, how they are born and die and are reborn different, through the permutation of their elements. And thus, we see the *whole*, where nothing is ever created out of nothing. And we can also see the gods, in their peaceful abodes, the gods who do not concern themselves with us and who are, for us, only models of a happy life.

Contents

Acknowledgments	9
Abbreviations	11
Introduction	15
1. Ponge and Plato	26
2. Ponge and the Bible	37
3. Ponge and Rameau	52
4. Ponge and Atomism	73
5. How the Text Rewrites its Atomic Structure	90
6. Lucretius and the Analogy of Atomic Texture	108
7. Cleansing the Textures	122
Conclusion	147
Notes	155
Works Cited	162
Index	167

Acknowledgments

I would like to express my sincere gratitude to the following people: Beth Archer Brombert, Victor Brombert, John Isbell, James Lawler, Rosemary Lloyd, Fabienne Meadows, Emanuel Mickel, Suzanne Nash, François Rigolot, Charles Segal, and Philip Watts. They offered comments and suggestions concerning this book from which I benefited a great deal.

The passages quoted from the writings of Francis Ponge are reproduced with the gracious permission of Editions Gallimard, Paris. "Francis Ponge: The Subversive Values of a Poetic Materialism," an earlier version of parts of chapters 1 and 2, appeared in Freeman G. Henry, ed., *Perceptions of Values,* French Literature Series vol. 22 (Amsterdam: Editions Rodopi, 1995), 57–66. An earlier version of chapter 3, entitled "Rameau and the Role of Music in Ponge's Poetry," was published in *The French Review* 68, no. 4 (March 1995): 626–37.

The photograph reproduced on the cover is by Patrick Meadows.

Abbreviations

The following abbreviations are used for some of the works of Francis Ponge referred to in this study:

AC = *L'Atelier contemporain* (Paris: Gallimard, 1977)
EPS = *Entretiens de Francis Ponge avec Philippe Sollers* (Paris: Gallimard/Editions du Seuil, 1970)
GRL = *Le Grand Recueil: Lyres* (Paris: Gallimard, 1961)
GRM = *Le Grand Recueil: Méthodes* (Paris: Gallimard, 1961)
GRP = *Le Grand Recueil: Pièces* (Paris: Gallimard, 1961)
N = *Nioque de l'Avant-Printemps* (Paris: Gallimard, 1983)
NR = *Nouveau Recueil* (Paris: Gallimard, 1967)
NRR = *Nouveau Nouveau Recueil,* 3 vols. (Paris: Gallimard, 1992)
PM = *Pour un Malherbe* (Paris: Gallimard, 1965)
S = *Le Savon* (Paris: Gallimard, 1967)
TP = *Tome premier* (Paris: Gallimard, 1965)

Francis Ponge
and the
Nature of Things

Introduction

The relationship between language and the world has fascinated thinkers since antiquity, and is one of the most prevalent topics of critical debate today. The works of the French poet Francis Ponge (1899–1988) are a refreshingly new exploration of this age-old philosophical problem, for they poetically combine ancient, modern, and idiosyncratic perspectives on the subject. Ponge is indeed best known for prose poems whose fundamental quality is a meditation on things of the external world and their relationship to language. Essential among the poet's recollections are those concerning what he calls the material as well as semantic "world" he perceived while contemplating the words in his father's Littré etymological dictionary (see Ponge 1970, 47–48).[1]

If Ponge, like Isidore of Seville in the Middle Ages, finds that the physical world is entirely incorporated in such a dictionary, it is because every word in it is defined by reference to other words' complete history of meaning and usage. Words talk about things by taking other words, and therefore other things, into account; and the Littré further considers words as they have appeared throughout the ages in other texts, thus providing what might be considered an all-inclusive chronicle of the various interrelations between things, words, thought, and expression. Ponge's work incorporates very detailed investigations of the dictionary, often actually reproducing articles from the Littré, thereby imparting to the reader a sense of the poet's "archaeological" movements among the matter of his language and those from which it derives.

Such materialistic perceptions, as they are continuously threaded throughout the poems, make Ponge's work very topical by placing it in a larger context: the ongoing semiotic discussion concerning language and referentiality, and the distinctions made between the elements of the linguistic sign.[2] The material aspect of the word, the signifier, receives a great deal of attention in his poetry, as does the signified, or the multiple references the word makes to other words, and not just to the things they denote.

The present book's goal, therefore, is to illuminate Ponge's poetry by exploring the interrelations between his work and materialistic philosophy, especially as expressed by Lucretius, and in this way to define his place better in the history of poetics. Although others have noticed this connection in his work, none has sufficiently shown exactly what in *De rerum natura* is so irresistibly attractive to Ponge, nor why, nor how Ponge's writings are nourished, and even shaped, by his use of the Latin poet's work and thought. This study seeks, within the general materialistic worldview so often said to underpin Ponge's project, a much more focused, more distinctively poetic point of interaction between thing and word, world and language, the natural construction of phenomena and the human construction of literary works.

Specific analogies in Lucretius's poem, as well as the particular cosmogonic principles that he inherited from Epicurus, are shown to animate the essential aspect of Ponge's poetics: the correlation between world and text. For Ponge, word and world are intertwined, and there are always two ways of understanding existence: words illuminate the world, and the world illuminates words. These two coexisting points of view join together to form the analogical core of his writings.

Many statements throughout Ponge's work lead us to believe that the author with whom he had the greatest affinities was the Roman poet Lucretius (c. 99–c. 55 B.C.), whose great didactic poem, *De rerum natura* (On the nature of things), expounds the atomistic theory of the Greek philosopher Epicurus. As Ponge himself said, he (unlike other contemporary poets) was not interested in composing separate poems, but aspired to the creation of a cohesive cosmogony: "Je voudrais écrire une sorte de *De natura rerum*"[3] [I would like to write a kind of *De rerum natura*] (*TP*, 200).[4] When pondering the "things" Ponge writes about, we therefore need to consider their relationship to the elements of all things, those primordial beginnings of things: the atoms. After all, Ponge himself insisted on the methodological importance of elementariness for his ethics and poetics: "Le plus simple est de reprendre tout du début, s'allonger sur l'herbe, et recommencer, comme si on ne savait rien" [The simplest way is to take up everything again from the beginning, lie down on the grass, and start over, as if one knew nothing] (*EPS*, 105).

His most famous collection, *Le Parti pris des choses* ([Taking] the side of things), first brought him recognition upon its publication in 1942. Even the title of this book made it clear that Ponge intended to break radically with the ancient lyric tradition, which he inherited most directly from its reincarnation in romanticism, by making objects of the external world, not emotional subjectivity, the topic of his texts. Indeed, this point of view is characteristic not only of *Le Parti pris des choses*, but of Ponge's entire work:

> "Les choses sont en selle, crie quelqu'un, et montent sur le genre humain de plus en plus." Tant mieux! lui répondrons-nous, la main sur le loquet de la porte. . . . Voici trop longtemps qu'elles nous tournaient le dos, tassées dans le fond de la cage où notre oeil, levé comme un fouet, les avait fait reculer! (*GRL*, 93)
>
> ["Things are in the saddle," somebody shouts, "and they are climbing up on the human race more and more." So much the better! we will respond, our hand on the door latch. . . . They had been turning their backs to us too long, crammed into the back of the cage where our eye, raised like a whip, had made them retreat.]

It is to things that Ponge wanted to give a voice, thereby rejecting the notion of the divinely or supernaturally inspired poet in order to focus on the pleasurable description-definition of the neglected phenomena of material existence. This typical reversal of poetic perspective indicates Ponge's effort to found a new humanism in which he hoped the individual and the world could be reconciled.[5]

In 1944, Jean-Paul Sartre's long essay on Ponge, "L'Homme et les choses," spurred critical interest.[6] Sartre's important analysis, which unfortunately could not take into consideration the numerous works to follow *Le Parti pris des choses*, aligns the poet's efforts with those of phenomenologists. Since then, a good deal of attention has been paid to this significant aspect of Ponge's work.

Although Alain Robbe-Grillet, himself a follower of phenomenology, while laying the theoretical foundation of the *nouveau roman* (new novel), insists on the incompatibilities of their styles and goals, similarities between Ponge and the new novelists have been noted.[7] Sartre further indicates Ponge's nominalism by saying that he had a "conception matérialiste du langage qui refuse de distinguer l'Idée du Verbe" [materialistic conception of language that refuses to distinguish between Idea and Word] (Sartre 1947, 229). Underscoring the link to ancient explanations of the world's origin, he uses a word of Ponge's idiolect when he calls his poetic enterprise a "cosmogony" (239); and, indeed, he refers to the specific relationship with Lucretius's cosmogony when he quotes Ponge, who declared *De rerum natura* to be the model of his project (239).

Surprisingly, however, Sartre's own brief, yet repeated observations regarding the poet's connection to materialism have to this day remained underdeveloped. This lacuna in Ponge criticism exists most probably because in his seminal essay, Sartre makes no mention of the specifically atomistic character of the poet's materialism. He fails to perceive the important analogical association that Lucretius establishes between matter and language, which is crucial for an understanding of Ponge's Epicureanism and, moreover, the importance for his work of *De rerum natura*. Despite the fact that several commentators have referred to Ponge's preoccupation with Epicurus and Lucretius, there is no book-length study of the association.

A veritable mine of information on a variety of topics including the poet's life and education, theory and practice, friendships with painters such as Picasso and Braque, discussions with poets such as Breton and Reverdy, and his place in literary tradition has been provided by Philippe Sollers. The prolific contemporary French novelist elucidates many aspects of Ponge's poetic enterprise by probing the poet's mind, successfully drawing him out with persistent perspicacity in not one, but a series of extensive sessions that were published in 1970 as a book-length volume entitled *Entretiens de Francis Ponge avec Philippe Sollers*. In addition to these interviews, Sollers's book entitled *Francis Ponge* (1963), and his views concerning the poet's efforts to create a new rhetoric, did much to spark the interest of many critics associated with the influential review *Tel Quel*, behind which Sollers himself was the driving force from 1960 to 1982. But the practically exclusive emphasis Sollers puts on Ponge's language, which he conceived of as lacking referentiality, vitiates to a certain degree any discussion of his materialistic poetics, which is founded not on an absolute divorce of words and things, but rather on their analogical relations. It is by virtue of these relations that Ponge attempts to delimit the specific difference of the things he writes about, both signs and referents.

By examining the many ways in which Ponge's signature becomes a text, his text a thing, and the thing his (its) signature, Jacques Derrida attempts to move beyond the two major directions taken so far by Ponge criticism (Derrida 1984, 23). The publication of his *Signéponge/Signsponge* in 1984 in a bilingual French/English edition added to Ponge's already considerable international reputation.[8] Extraordinarily Pongian in its punning, the title of this compelling analysis of the filigree signature is loaded with ambiguity: "Signed Ponge," "Sign and Ponge," and "Sign-sponge" are three compartments of the densely packed portmanteau word *signéponge*, the portmanteau word being a technique used to a considerable extent by Ponge himself in his effort to remotivate the linguistic sign in keeping with what he called "the semantic density of words." According to Derrida, since a movement toward the outside (a phenomenological return to things themselves) and a movement toward the inside (a theoretical return to the question of language's role in literature) constitute a symmetrical opposition in the critical approaches to Ponge's work, there is no longer any reason to be satisfied with either one (24). But this objection does not prove that there is sufficient reason to leave these approaches behind, since a third critical direction remains, which has not yet been sufficiently explored and which, moreover, is implied by the very opposition that Derrida points out. Instead of leaving these major critical directions disconnected and opposed, it is possible and desirable to seek their mutual resolution in a movement toward the middle where they overlap, neither in the law of the thing, nor in the law of the word, but in a link that both Lucretius and Ponge use to combine them, a connection coexistent with poetry itself: analogy, whose structure encourages the resolution of opposites, of singularity and difference. Indeed, Ponge himself formulated the importance of this middle ground: "PARTI PRIS DES CHOSES *égale* COMPTE TENU DES MOTS" [{TAKING}[9] THE SIDE OF THINGS *equals* TAKING WORDS INTO ACCOUNT] (*GRM*, 19). Such a resolution is therefore already embedded in the poet's work, but its elucidation requires a focused definition of the link between Ponge and Lucretius, especially as concerns the question of analogy.

※ ※ ※

Many critics of Ponge have dubbed him a "materialist" poet, and have noticed that Lucretius seems to be the guarantor of this philosophy in his work. In fact, this link, which Ponge did not keep secret, has been pointed out so frequently that mentioning each critic who has done so would be unnecessarily repetitious. Brief reference to a select few should nevertheless help inform the reader regarding the critical background and direction of this study.

Not unlike Sartre, Jean-Pierre Richard, in his essay entitled "Francis Ponge," which is a chapter of his book *Onze études sur la poésie moderne,* writes that "dans chaque objet, il vise à dégager non point vraiment l'idée (ce mot n'appartient pas à son vocabulaire, et Ponge s'affirme, assez curieusement, matérialiste), mais la ou les qualités" [in each object, his aim is not really to reveal the idea (this word does not belong to his vocabulary, and Ponge asserts, oddly enough, that he is a materialist), but the quality or qualities] (1964, 206). Richard, however, makes no attempt to analyze Ponge's connection to Epicurus or Lucretius, and therefore we do not learn how these "qualities" of words are illuminated by the poet's appropriation of his precursors.

The materialist strain of Ponge's work inevitably requires us to consider him within the history of ideas. So states Marcel Spada (1979, 5), who developed this observation by pointing out that Ponge "a pu trouver chez le plus grand poète latin [i.e., Lucrèce] le phare d'une doctrine" [was able to find in the greatist Latin poet (i.e., Lucretius) the guiding light of a doctrine], while at the same time drawing our attention to the poet's cautiousness regarding the epithet "scientific" attached to materialism: Ponge challenged rationalistic imperialism, although, according to Spada, at times scientific discourse does collaborate with his poetry (9). One of the most profound studies to date concerning the materialist aspect of Ponge's work, Spada's essay "Francis Ponge au corps des lettres," in his book *Francis Ponge*, further maintains that, as far as the poet's view of humanity is concerned, "c'est . . . en référence à Epicure que Ponge ne voit pas en l'homme un être à l'âme spirituelle et immortelle, mais un élément de qualité à remplacer dans le grand cycle de l'univers" [it is . . . in reference to Epicurus that, in man, Ponge does not see a being with a spiritual and immortal soul, but a qualitative element to replace in the great cycle of the universe] (11). For Spada, the healing effect of Ponge's approach to poetry stands out: "Dans l'objet, il recherche d'abord le point d'amarrage, la borne indispensable contre les vertiges métaphysiques" [In the object, he looks first for the moorings, the indispensable limits against metaphysical vertigo] (12). This critic asserts that Ponge's ethics "nous ramène à Epicure pour qui philosopher, c'est d'abord vivre—et vivre heureux" [takes us back to Epicurus for whom to philosophize is first to live—and live happily] (13); and he sees the proof of this in what Jean Paulhan, recalling Epicurus's ataraxia (peace of mind, emotional tranquility), describes as the "sérénité rayonnante" [radiating serenity] of Ponge's *Le Parti pris des choses* (12). Moreover, the many erotic themes in Ponge's writings may, as Spada believes, have as their source the apostrophe to Venus "qui met en branle [l]e *De Natura*" [which sets the *De rerum natura* in motion] (18). Spada, however, neglects the fact that what is set in motion here is an explanation of the atomic nature of things, and that, therefore, the mythical Venus is a metaphor of the natural creative processes that constitute Lucretius's real topic.

Ian Higgins, like Spada, underlines the ethical content of Ponge's work as it relates to Epicureanism. On the first page of his *Francis Ponge* (1979), Higgins presents the poet as an "Epicurean materialist," and he returns to materialism later in the book. He points out, for instance, that Ponge's association with Georges Braque's art work—which, in Ponge's essays on the painter, illustrates an emphasis on practice analogous to his own—is related to his "aspiring to what Lucretius, the Epicurean materialist, called *sapientia*, a lucid, modest, mature wisdom," in which "harmonious relations between the individual and the outside world" are achieved (1979, 108–9). But he does not point out that, in Epicureanism, the ethics is the point of arrival, not of departure: atomistic physics is the necessary beginning that ultimately rids humans of the fear of divine intervention, thus leading to ataraxia. Given the emphasis Ponge continually places on elementariness, on beginnings, the connection of his work to the physics must be made clear before we can talk about his Epicurean ethics.

In the critical introduction to his fine translations of a selection of Ponge's poems, *The Power of Language,* Serge Gavronsky, echoing points made by both Sartre and Richard, asserts that "Ponge limits his philosophic engagements to material definitions, a form of nominalism" (1979, 14). Like Spada, Gavronsky states that "the writings of Epicurus, and especially their poetic interpretation in . . . *De natura rerum*" might be the antecedent of Ponge's approach to poetry, and he appropriately reminds us that Ponge himself expresses his ambition "to duplicate Lucretius's own methodological approach to the universe, to the universe of language, too" (14). But what exactly is Lucretius's approach to the universe and to language? Does Ponge really "duplicate" it, or is the appropriation accompanied by remotivation? Do Lucretius and Ponge talk about precisely the same thing?

In spite of the references to the connection between Ponge's work and materialism, which dot many studies devoted to the poet, even recent criticism emphasizes the work in this area that still needs to be undertaken. Bernard Beugnot, in the conclusion of his book *Poétique de Francis Ponge,* insists that "tout le matériau venu de la tradition avec lequel il travaille" [all the traditional material with which he works] has not yet been examined (1990, 203). Foremost on Beugnot's list of such material is Lucretius's poem, which not only "sert de caution à la philosophie matérialiste et à l'épicurisme moral" [acts as a guarantee of materialistic philosophy and moral Epicureanism], but also, as Spada suggests, "inspire très directement l'imaginaire érotique" [very directly inspires the erotic imagination] of his poetry (204). Most importantly, Beugnot maintains that, for Ponge, "l'épopée de la création qu'est le *De natura rerum* s'offre comme modèle de l'appropriation du monde" [the epic of creation that is *De rerum natura* presents itself as a model of the appropriation of the world] (204); and yet his comment is meant to identify lacunae in Ponge criticism, including his own book.

Along with the contributions of Sartre, Sollers, and Derrida, the studies that have just been discussed provide ample proof of contemporary philosophers', artists', and critics' esteem for the poet. Indeed, the public's interest can be expected to increase even more in the near future, since Ponge's complete works are soon to be gathered together for the first time in the prestigious Gallimard edition, *Bibliothèque de la Pléiade*.

※ ※ ※

All the criticism discussed above has played a significant role in the preparation of this book, and I am grateful to the authors mentioned, and others as well, for having stimulated my own reflections. But perhaps most important for the present study has been the commentary on Ponge's work that was made by Michael Riffaterre. This critic has shown that Ponge's poetic constructions may be understood in terms of a process of expansion from a core, or *mot-noyau*, which contains the text's virtual formal and semantic developments (see Riffaterre 1977, 66). My critical approach incorporates this observation while modifying it in consideration of Ponge's atomistic perspective. In a way that constitutes a critical parallel to Ponge's own textual expansion, I demonstrate that not only do his writings derive their qualities from a "kernel-word," but also from various intellectual confrontations or encounters with prior philosophers' and artists' visions of the world, poetry, music, and their interrelations. His poetics emphasizes the creative function of analogy (in the nuanced sense of proportion, not just similarity) in the development of a poetic language capable of expressing the nature of texts in relation to the external world of nature, as well as to the homologous world of literature. It is in this world that he would have his work take its place; the material to which he refers and which he uses in his own writings is therefore often derived from other works that make up this textual world. My analyses show that the reader perceives Ponge in the process of not only expanding but also distilling elements from these intertexts in order to refashion them subsequently into his own project, and, further, that this process of textual construction is analogous to the mechanisms of nature to which the poet frequently refers.

Two analogies that Lucretius invoked in order to explain the atomic nature of things will concern us especially. They have not been chosen arbitrarily: both inform the cornerstone of Ponge's poetics as defined above. Lucretius poeticized Epicurus's thought by comparing atoms to the letters of the alphabet.[10] According to his analogy, as individual combinations of letters produce the variety of words in language, so particular arrangements of atoms give rise to distinct things in the external world. The same Latin word that means "atoms" in Lucretius's explanation also signifies "letters": *elementa*, elements. Both the world of phenomena and the world of language exist through the permutation of their elements. We therefore find the same fundamental analogy linking world and language, things and words, in our poet's precursor, whose project he claimed as a model. I examine this analogy as it reappears in Ponge's dialogues—sometimes subversive, sometimes corroborative—with Plato, the Bible, Jean-Philippe Rameau. This study further establishes a historical and philosophical horizon of expectation based on the literary tradition of learned poetry *(poésie scientifique);* Ponge's poetic cosmogony is defined within the parameters of the atomistic tradition, with the acknowledgment of intellectual contributions both from prescientific and modern perspectives.

Subsequent chapters discuss Ponge's semantic notion of "text," concentrating on his reuse of the Lucretian comparison of atomic construction to weaving. Like the analogy atom-letter, this analogy joins natural and human activity: the way in which atoms are interconnected within the things of the external world is illustrated by reference to the structure of textiles. In many instances, this analogy is extended metaphorically by Ponge to include the creation of texts: the etymologies of many words used figuratively to designate literary phenomena reveal a fundamental connection to the art of weaving, such as the noun *text* (*texte* in French), which derives from the Latin *textus*, woven thing, and ultimately from *texere*, to weave. As is common practice for Ponge, his reading of Lucretius takes the historical development of such words into consideration and exploits it in his cosmogony of the textual phenomenon.

※ ※ ※

Behind this book lies another book: the second part of a diptych concerning the work of Ponge and materialism. In agreement with T. S. Eliot's idea that all texts coexist in a timeless or simultaneous order[11]—an opinion often expressed by Ponge himself—I have chosen to examine ancient sources before moving on to more recent developments, such as Marxism. Indeed, in this respect, it is worth remembering that the subject of Marx's own doctoral thesis was entitled "The Difference between the Democritean and Epicurean Philosophy of Nature" (in Marx 1967); this illustrates a willed continuity between past and present aspects of the materialistic tradition.

The study of the link between Ponge's work and Marxism, to pick only one of the most striking modern avatars of materialism, is complicated by the fact that, although Ponge had a generally favorable view of Marx and the social goals of his political doctrine, he was reluctant to proclaim dialectical materialism as a philosophical interpretation of all reality. As Ponge himself remarked, Marxist political action has great powers of self-propagation,

> Mais seulement dans la mesure où elle reste action, nullement dans la mesure où elle se fait thèse, philosophie ou critique dans l'absolu. Car elle perd alors tout pouvoir, toute vertu. Dans cette seconde mesure, elle agit comme son propre frein.... ("La Seine," in *TP*, 553)
>
> [But only to the extent that it remains action, not at all to the extent that it becomes a thesis, philosophy or critique in the absolute. For then it loses all power, all virtue. In this second case, it acts as its own brake....]

Nevertheless, this statement expresses above all Ponge's personal choice as it relates to his own writings; it certainly does not mean to suggest that others should refrain from expressing their particular points of view. Authors, of course, never have the last say on their works, and it seems to me that a subsequent volume on Ponge and materialism should situate itself within the long-standing debate between Marxist and existentialist views of the object and objectification, a debate that was crystallizing precisely in the period prior to Ponge's earliest writings. Such a study would examine the question of things, their properties, and their relations to people who use or perceive them, a topic that enthralled not only Ponge but also the entire modernist sensibility, from the rejection of abstraction that was urged by Pound to the collecting of objects that was practiced by the surrealists. Indeed, objects had assumed an almost religious status for the surrealists, and the futurist movement, with Marinetti at the helm, had sketched in a poetics of matter nearly thirty years before Ponge. The study could also encompass the relation between Ponge's work and certain movements in the plastic arts, such as the "anti-art" of Marcel Duchamp, whose readymades consisted of ordinary objects ironically promoted to the rank of art, or currents in twentieth-century music, like Luigi Russolo's project for an "art of noises," a music in which every kind of sound would be valued for its materiality, not its communicative or spiritualizing powers.

All of these literary and artistic movements can and should be explored in connection with the work of Ponge in order to clarify its place in the entire project of literary modernism and its aftermath. But, as in my view this needs to be done within the context of materialistic philosophy and its evolution, the present study will focus on the sources of the poet's worldview as reflected in his understanding and use of the ancient Greek atomism of

Epicurus and its expression in the poetry of Lucretius. This study indicates that it is in his simultaneous conserving and remodeling of Lucretius that Ponge is truly modern. Ponge is modern, not in spite of his connection to ancient tradition, but thanks to it. The newest things, whether phenomena of the external world or of the literary world, always owe their existence to the atoms or elements that they absorb and remotivate. Ponge's work, in that it intentionally presents itself as linked analogically and "genealogically" (Ponge would say "geneanalogically") to Lucretius, imitates this ubiquitous natural and literary rhythm. Whereas Lucretius had invoked words—the elements of textual phenomena—in order to explain the texture of the world and to rid the human race of its fear regarding divine intervention, Ponge often reverses the proportion, calling on the interwoven atomic world depicted by Lucretius in his effort to describe and define the predominant subject of the modern poem: linguistic elements and their role in the texture of poetry, that is, the poetic text itself. He thus develops the metaphorical foundation on which his ethical endeavor to "cleanse" words takes shape. Language being defined, thanks to the link with Lucretius, as a textile product, Ponge may proceed to what he calls the "toilette intellectuelle" of words (intellectual washing, with an etymological pun on the word *toile*, which derives from the Latin *tela*, web). In so doing, he intends to rid words of meanings divisive to, and restore to them associations supportive of, the reconciliation between humans and the world to which he so fervently aspires.

1
Ponge and Plato

In the conclusion of his book on Francis Ponge, Bernard Beugnot points out that contemporary criticism has tended to overlook the traditional material with which the poet works (1990, 203). Such a lacuna in studies concerning this undeniably central figure of modern French letters is truly regrettable.[1] Exploration of the link to the ancients is necessary in order to sharpen the well-established view that Ponge is a materialist, especially as his views concerning the world, literature, and their interrelations derive, in the main, from ancient Greek atomism and its expression in the poetry of Lucretius. At the threshold of a study concerning the ways in which Ponge uses and remotivates some of his precursors in an effort to set forth his own poetic theory and practice, I would like to examine the dialogue with an aspect of the literary and philosophical tradition with which Ponge's work is engaged: the dichotomy of idealistic and materialistic notions of poetry.[2]

Clearly at odds with idealism, Francis Ponge, by means of the very images developed in his work, encourages his readers to question any and all notions of poetry that derive from this philosophy, be they ancient or modern. Dissatisfied with the idealistic framework in general because, in his view, it tends to restrict poetic discourse to "acceptable" topics and consequently makes the work of some poets unacceptable, he claims that legitimate poetic subjects include things that are not ordinarily thought of as "poetic." Indeed, if considered from a traditional point of view, the subjects of Ponge's poetry are the most prosaic of things, and therefore by definition not fit for the lofty domain of poetry. In this regard, one may think of the revealing titles of texts from *Le Parti pris des choses*, like "Le Cageot" (The crate), "Le Pain" (The loaf of bread), and "Le galet" (The pebble).[3]

Often represented as material phenomena and their processes, the function of the poet and the nature of poetry, far from being defined by their

1 / Ponge and Plato

relationship to a specific divinity, are compared by Ponge to the universal dynamism of the physical world. By overthrowing prior idealistic representations of the poet as inspired by a supernatural being, and by insisting instead on poetry's analogical association with the external world, Ponge's writings, although very modern in their expression, provide a bridge to ancient, materialistic explanations of the world's origin and manner of functioning, and in particular to Lucretius's poetic interpretation of Epicurus's atomistic philosophy in his *De rerum natura*. As Ponge himself has said:

> Je voudrais écrire une sorte de *De natura rerum*. On voit bien la différence avec les poètes contemporains: ce ne sont pas des poèmes que je veux composer, mais une seule cosmogonie. (*Proêmes*, in *TP*, 200)
>
> [I would like to write a kind of *De rerum natura*. The difference between other contemporary poets and me is clear: it is not poems that I want to compose, but a single cosmogony.]

Ponge's readers inevitably encounter his particular notion of poetry, since, as illustrated by the passage quoted above, his writings actually take the concept of poetry as their subject. Perhaps his disparaging remarks concerning the notion of "poet" should be interpreted not as a denial of poetic qualities in his work, but as an attempt to warn his readers by distinguishing between his views and those of others concerning the role and the product of the poet: "Le jour où l'on voudra bien admettre . . . que je ne me veux pas poète, . . . on s'épargnera bien des discussions oiseuses à mon sujet" [The day when people willingly admit . . . that I am not striving to be a poet, . . . they will spare themselves many useless discussions about me] ("My Creative Method," in *GRM*, 40–41). The very fact that he takes issue with the word *poet* encourages us to reflect on what it has meant in the past, and what it may possibly mean now and in the future. According to a certain idea of poetry, he may very well not be a poet, whereas he may nevertheless be a poet of another poetry that he strives to develop.

In "My Creative Method"—possibly his most revealing metapoetic work—Ponge defines the kind of poet he is, and the type of poetry he writes, by quoting at length the well-known passage from Plato's *Apology* in which Socrates relates his conversations with poets, as well as other artists and artisans (*GRM*, 28–31). These discussions were part of a vain attempt to find someone having knowledge greater than his own. Socrates concluded that, although their sayings were beautiful, poets could not explain their own poems, since they were not guided by reason, but by inspiration. Ponge, commenting on this passage, says that Socrates would never have asked for an explanation if the poems had contained within themselves their own "évidence": a justification that is readily available to sensory perception. But in this case, he adds, one might wonder whether they would have still been called poems (31). These pages clearly express Ponge's opposition to the kind of poetry that, he believes, is best exemplified by the Platonic notion of poetic enthusiasm: it denies reason to poets and therefore implies that, unaided by the divinity, they are incapable of revealing the *Logos* (in the Greek philosophical sense) through their own personal arrangement of linguistic elements. Ponge, on the other hand, has countered by asserting that *le Verbe* is not received from an extralinguistic source, but is proffered by the poet's skillful manipulation of the material aspect of language itself, through which the universal principle or meaningful structure of reality becomes manifest (see *PM,* 142–44, 184, 215).

If Ponge is nevertheless a poet, it is thanks to a conception of poetry that relocates us all—the poet, you, and me—on level ground, within the phenomenal world, without stranding a "privileged" chosen few halfway between metaphysical "reality" and here below. Words such as *inspiration, possession,* or *genius* cannot really be applied to Ponge and his work unless some irony is intended. What "inspires" him is not capable of inspiring as it was understood according to a tradition that, with the possible exception of Musset and Lamartine, had already been reduced to figurative, metaphorical statements with the romantics. Since he obtains the impetus to write from the things of the phenomenal world, the ancient notion of poetic enthusiasm is of equally little relevance here. Things in nature, unlike muses, gods, or demons, can neither solicit a person's approval nor approve or reject an individual: "Nous . . . ne tenons la parole que du monde muet, notre seule patrie. . . . Elle n'a jamais proscrit personne" [We . . . receive speech from the mute world alone, our only homeland. . . . It has never exiled anybody] (*PM*, 31).

As illustrated by the passage quoted above, in his *Pour un Malherbe* (For a Malherbe)—a genuine *ars poetica*—Ponge emphasizes his role as an element in a social group. One way in which he does so throughout the work is by consistently using the first-person plural subject pronoun, *nous.* This intentionally creates a contrast between his poetics and romanticism, in which the first-person singular pronoun was typical; and it suggests that Ponge consciously thinks of himself not only as a distinct individual expressing his own thoughts and emotions, but also as a functioning part of a human collectivity including both author and readers.[4]

Ponge attempts to unify poet and readers by conceiving of poetry not as the mysterious finished product of an isolated genius, but as an ongoing activity or collaborative enterprise involving each one of us, as in this parody of the Cartesian *cogito ergo sum*: "Puisque tu me lis, cher lecteur, donc je suis; puisque tu nous lis (mon livre et moi), cher lecteur, donc nous sommes (Toi, lui et moi)" [Since you read me, dear reader, therefore I am; since you read us (my book and me), dear reader, therefore we are (You, it, and I)] (*PM*, 203).[5] Rather than understanding poetry as the exclusive domain of a favored few, Ponge sees it as the cooperative creation of a variety of distinct, yet integrated, elements. These elements are characterized not only by their acting as subjects, as in Descartes's definition of his own existence, but also by their being acted on as objects. Ponge refuses any notion of the poet's role (no matter how apparently flattering) that would distance him from his material and social surroundings; and thus, just as we, his readers, are neither more nor less a part of the pronoun *nous* than he is, he is neither more nor less an inhabitant of this world than we are. In that others are as important to his existence as he is to theirs, such a poet may be understood as a reconciler.

Poetry as an act of reconciliation is by no means a recent notion. The concept can certainly be traced back at least as far as the idealism of Plato. Supposing that the essence of the poetic act is correctly defined as residing in some kind of reconciliation, what then is the relationship between Ponge's conceptualization of his writings and this notion? How does his view of poetry interrelate with, or modify, the avatars of poetic reconciliation that have appeared throughout the ages?

Given that he is a materialist, and that, as Beugnot reminds us, the guarantor of this philosophy in his work is the ancient Epicurean philosopher and poet Lucretius, to whom Ponge himself often refers, it would be surprising if, while developing his views concerning his own materialistic poetry, Ponge did not also refer to representatives of ancient idealism, thus inviting his readers to contrast the very different ways in which these opposing world-views conceive of poetry. His work would thereby appropriate the prestige of the authors to whom he alludes in order to undermine them all the more effectively. Since Ponge does indeed refer to Socrates in an effort to define his own kind of poetry, my response to this invitation will be to devote the remainder of my discussion to a comparison between two symbolic images of poetry as such, the one ancient and idealistic, the other modern and materialistic: Plato's chain and Ponge's tree.

In Plato's work, the function of the poet is defined as being that of a mediator, not between human beings, nor between the human race and nature, but between divinity and humanity. Here, Socrates speaks to the rhapsode Ion:

SOCRATES. This gift you have of speaking well on Homer is not an art; it is a power divine, impelling you like the power in the stone Euripides called the Magnet, which most call "stone of Hercules." This stone does not simply attract the iron rings, just by themselves; it also imparts to the rings a force enabling them to do the same thing as the stone itself, that is, to attract another ring, so that sometimes a chain is formed, quite a long one, of iron rings, suspended one from another. For all of them, however, their power depends on that lodestone. Just so the Muse. She first makes men inspired, and then through these inspired ones, others share in the enthusiasm, and a chain is formed. . . . Herein lies the reason why the Deity has bereft them of their senses, and uses them as ministers, along with soothsayers and godly seers; it is in order that we listeners may know that it is not they who utter these precious revelations while their mind is not within them, but that it is the God himself who speaks, and through them becomes articulate to us. (Plato 1938, 82–84)

The importance of this idea in the historical development of the concept of poetry is well known. The romantic notion of "genius" is in part derived from it; and it may be owing to such Platonic explanations that lofty isolation came to be associated with poets. This very isolation was understood as being glorious in that it was a quality evoked by the laudatory word *genius*. Glorious, because the genius, inspired by something intangible, beyond the relatively confined experience of common individuals, "sees" what they do not: unlike Ponge, the poets in Socrates' example receive speech from a metaphysical being who authorizes their voices only, thereby distinguishing them among humans. The role of the poet, according to this view, is that of a reconciler between ordinary and transcendent existence, a glimpse of which we receive from the poet who serves a muse. By implication, unlike Ponge's homeland (the world of things), the inspiring muse (the homeland of Socrates' poet) both chooses and in a sense exiles some people, since poets participate to a greater degree than others in the essence of the spirit who speaks through them. Their allegiance is owed to this spiritual essence, and thus only to a lesser extent to the world in which the rest of us live. Indeed, it is this sense of separation that justifies the poet's role of mediator: given that we are not poets, the rest of us know full well by comparison just how far we are from divinity.

Whereas in the example from Plato's *Ion*, Socrates represents poetry as a magnetized chain, in his *Pour un Malherbe*, Ponge's notion of poetry is rendered by the image of a tree:

Nous jugerions oiseux d'ajouter un livre à la bibliothèque concernant un vieil auteur de notre littérature nationale, s'il ne *s'y* agissait, dans notre esprit, de bêcher un peu au pied de l'arbre, pour lui permettre de respirer et de s'élever encore.

 Naturellement, c'est la cime de cet arbre qui nous intéresse, c'est-à-dire la littérature *présente*, comme elle pousse des feuilles dans le ciel de l'avenir. (*PM*, 189)

[We would consider it pointless to add a book about an old author of our national literature {i.e., Malherbe} to the library, if, in our mind, it were not a question of hoeing a bit at the foot of the tree, thereby allowing it to breathe and grow some more.

 Naturally, it is the top of this tree that interests us, that is, the literature *of today*, as its leaves shoot up toward the sky of the future.]

He describes himself as a leaf on the tree of French language and literature, and asserts that Malherbe is the trunk. For Ponge, Malherbe is the paradigmatic French writer, the founder of all subsequent French letters worthy of esteem, including Ponge's own contribution. This is so because Malherbe is "le modèle des classiques" [the model of the classics] (*PM*, 33), and, as such, is comparable to an indispensable material element and eternal principle. Malherbe is in fact represented by a series of interrelated metaphors: "la vibration de la basse fondamentale" [the vibration of the fundamental bass] (143) of a musical composition; the corner stone of French literature: "Otez Malherbe de l'édifice littéraire français, tout s'écroule" [Remove Malherbe from the French literary edifice, everything collapses] (83); the kernel or atomic nucleus of the French language: "c'est son noyau le plus dur, le plus indestructible" [he is its hardest and most indestructible nucleus] (242). Ponge sees Malherbe's work—in opposition, for example, to the effusive poetry of the Pléiade—as a forebear with regard to his own writings; he continues and develops the solid, careful and moderate restraint that he admires in Malherbe.[6] Along with the metaphors mentioned above, the image of the tree—one of the most prevalent images of Malherbe— also expresses this point of view: "Malherbe fait partie de mon propre bois, si je puis dire. Il a été intimement lié à ma substance durant ma croissance même et s'y est intégré" [Malherbe is part of my own wood, so to say. He was intimately bound to my matter even as I was growing, and has become an integral part of it] (36). Malherbe as the trunk and Ponge as the leaf are interconnected but coexistent; they have different yet reciprocal functions. Malherbe is as dependent on Ponge as Ponge is on Malherbe. Ponge sings the praises of Malherbe, but he does so with his own very original voice.

 According to Socrates, however, the chain of poetry is an accurate representation since poets lack originality: it is not their voice we hear, but that of a metaphysical being who uses them as ministers. Consequently, poetry is disseminated by interpreters of poets, or rhapsodes, such as Ion, who have even less individuality: they are, as Socrates says, "possessed" and therefore they interpret poets such as Homer, who are themselves interpreters of a muse (Plato 1938, 85). For Socrates then, poetry is already interpretation, and the role of the rhapsodes is that of "interpreters of interpreters" (84). Accordingly, Homer, in the image of the magnetized chain, is a primary ring, whereas Ion, and other interpreters of Homer, are suspended, secondary rings.

In Socrates' scheme, all the links in the chain following the primary must be imitative and therefore subordinate to it. The function of the secondary rings, or rhapsodes, is essentially one of repetition. Only the initial ring—the poet proper—might seem to possess some originality, simply by virtue of its being the first. But even this modicum of originality disappears when one considers that the poets too are deprived of their judgment by the inspiring god.

The latter elements in the Platonic chain, for instance, are said to depend entirely on the primary link (e.g., Homer). Never is there a hint that some kind of reciprocal or balanced interdependence based on different, individual qualities or functions is required to maintain the viability of the chain: the transmission of power takes place forever along a single, descending path. The power transmitter never requires recharging by means of a return of power. It is never a question of Ion sending force back to Homer. Since Socrates points out that poets are the first rings connected to their particular deity and that others are "suspended" from these initial rings, it seems that the chain is presented as descending. Yet this descent is not really meant to represent a movement of things in general from being to becoming, these two realms being separate in Plato's system. Rather, it illustrates only the nature of the soul, which partakes of both the world of the idea and the world of appearances (see Cassirer 1963, 125). It is through the vehicle of poetry, as presented here, that the soul's movement is exemplified, for Plato's notion of poetry parallels his conception of the human being.

In his *Timaeus*, for instance, Plato represents the human being as a tree, only here the image is inverted: the tree's roots are not in the earth, but in the heavens, "for it is to the heavens, whence the soul first came to birth, that the divine part attaches the head or root of us and keeps the whole body upright" (Plato 1937, 353). For Plato, then, the images of the tree and of the chain express much the same philosophical point of view. Both images constitute variations on a single theme: the human being's place "below" archetypal reality. Although the magnetized chain is made of a series of hanging rings, the significance of the image lies in the lodestone's power to attract: it produces an upward movement toward the idea.

Ponge, however, sees the human being and poetry differently. Accordingly, his tree, like trees in the exterior world, grows from the earth toward the sky. But for Ponge, the tree's growth does not symbolize the soul's tendency toward metaphysical reality, nor any communion between humanity and divinity. In order to reverse the ancient, idealistic metaphor of the sky, which expresses the inferior materiality of earth in relation to the heavens, Ponge ironically transforms the expression *ici-bas* (here below) into *ici-haut* (here above), thereby communicating his opposition to the worldview it suggests: his ethical stance, as was the case for Epicurus and Lucretius, involves neither good nor evil spirits: "Fraternité et bonheur (ou plutôt joie virile): voilà le seul ciel où j'aspire. Ici-haut" [Fraternity and happiness (or rather virile joy): that is the only heaven to which I aspire. Here above] (*Proêmes*, in *TP*, p. 214). In this passage, furthermore, the phrase "le seul ciel" [the only heaven] is remarkable: the adjective "seul" implies that another heaven exists, but that to it *this* one is preferred. As a result, the passage expresses Ponge's grudge against metaphysics.

By requiring the reader to ponder words whose meanings are ordinarily taken for granted, the passage further reveals Ponge's effort to draw words such as *ciel* and *aspirer* away from exclusively idealistic connotations in order to give them fresh significance in the context of a materialistic poetics and ethics: the earth is not inferior to the "sky," because both are essentially material; and if there is an "ideal" to which we may aspire, it is to be found only here, among humans, and not in the heavens: "Il faut que l'homme, tout comme d'abord le poète, trouve sa loi, sa clef, son dieu en lui-même" [Human beings, just as initially the poet, must find their law, their key, their god within themselves] (*Proêmes*, in *TP*, 216). Instead of beginning in a metaphysical being, the roots of poetry, as illustrated by the image of the tree, are in the material world in which we actually exist and operate as bodies among other bodies, and where this very interaction is our significance.

Whether idealist or materialist, the poet as mediator is located somewhere between parts of an interconnecting system. Following Plato, Homer is between a god and humans. According to Ponge, however, Malherbe is between the roots and the leaves of the tree, or, analogously, between the Latin materialistic poet whose work Ponge has claimed as a model and Ponge himself: when he speaks of Malherbe's place in literary history, Ponge insists that "il faut . . . le situer à peu près aux trois quarts du chemin sur la route qui mène de Lucrèce à moi" [one must . . . place him at about three-quarters distance along the road that leads from Lucretius to me] (*PM*, 262). Malherbe, far from connecting a god and human beings, is the author whose sensitivity to the material aspect of words, whose "concert de vocables, de sons *significatifs*" [concert of vocables, of *meaningful* sounds] (*PM*, 137, 149) constitutes the "transposition" of the Lucretian roots into French soil, where, to the benefit of generations to come, it can be carried forth into "the sky of the future" by the Pongian leaf.

Reconciliation, not between heaven and earth, but between humans, and between humans and nature—individuals participating in the material world, the world of things—is what, from Ponge's point of view, is most worthy of interest. Our function is to exercise our unique linguistic power, to be the valuable element by which the fascinating yet overlooked universe of phenomena is given expression:

> Ce galet gagna la victoire (la victoire de l'existence, individuelle, concrète, la victoire de me tomber sous les yeux et de naître à la parole) parce qu'il est plus intéressant que le ciel. ("My Creative Method," in *GRM*, 26–27)

> [This pebble won the victory (the victory of existence, individual, concrete, the victory of being noticed by me and of being born into speech) because it is more interesting than the sky.]

Whereas the poet in the idealistic framework seeks to reconcile us with what we cannot see, that is, an invisible spirit—"le ciel" (the sky)—Ponge reconciles us with what we see but tend to find unworthy of poetic contemplation: the common things that surround us, here on earth, for even a pebble is not beneath us.

Ponge's readers rightly see his art as a reconciliatory path leading to their reintegration into the natural world, the welfare of which depends on their active participation as an element in it. Things may be said to implore reconciliation not through their participation in the Platonic ontological continuum between symbolizer and symbolized, but thanks to their enigmatic quality, which, like any salutary creative constraint, challenges the poet. Once expressed in our world of language, their very difference illumines the structures of our thought, and in this way reconciles them and us.

Accordingly, Ponge's work actually insists on the reader's active participation by emphasizing the analogy between his writings and the things of the external world, as in his image of the tree. Ponge has indeed defined the very existence of his poetry as dependent on its being read, and he has further maintained that the act of reading is the basis of the reader's own existence. Ponge's tree of French language and literature—so very different in this respect from Socrates' chain—is the supplier of the reader's "air"; and it is Ponge, among others, as a leaf of the tree, whose specific function is the creation of the oxygen thanks to which the reader can breathe. Both poet and reader, far from dominating nature, actually participate as physical elements in it, and thereby bring about the desired reconciliation between nature and humans. As Ponge himself expresses it: "Il suffit d'abaisser notre prétention à dominer la nature et d'élever notre prétention à en faire physiquement partie, pour que la réconciliation ait lieu" [Lowering our ambition to dominate nature and raising our ambition to be a physical part of it is all that is needed in order to bring about the reconciliation] ("Le Monde muet est notre seule patrie," in *GRM*, 197).

Unlike Plato's image, which is located in the mineral realm of the inanimate magnet, Ponge's tree, being a biological organism, lends itself to the representation of the poetic function as irrevocably connected to the bodily processes involved in linguistic acts. The poet and the reader, after all, are biological entities; and the passages from *Pour un Malherbe* quoted above, instead of linking poetry to divine inspiration, clearly associate the vegetal and human physiological processes of *respiration*, thus bringing about the desired poetic reconciliation. It is the tree of poetry that creates the element necessary to both the reader's physiological and intellectual life. The role of the poet, as expressed by Ponge's image of the tree, is therefore the production of *oxygène* (oxygen), which, in French, signifies at once a chemical element necessary to respiration and the figurative "souffle nouveau" (new breath) necessary not only to the continued growth of the literary tree but also to the dynamism of those readers living in the intellectual atmosphere that, with Ponge's contribution, it provides.

Perhaps the most significant difference revealed by the comparison of Plato's chain and Ponge's tree concerns the role of the poet. According to Ponge's views, the poet's allegiance is owed not to the suprasensory realm of ideas, but only to the physical world: no one—neither the poet nor anyone else—is banished from the source of Ponge's writings. It is he who chooses to serve as the voice of mute things, and has therefore not been singled out among humans by a supernatural being to perform as an inspired medium: this is why Ponge would certainly appear not to be a poet, if one's definition of *poet* were established by an idealistic context, represented, for example, by Plato. But since from this point of view it is not really the poets who speak, but the muse who, thanks to their neutrality, speaks through them, their function in relation to poetry is, from Ponge's point of view, impersonal, objective, and quantitative. On the other hand, Ponge's relationship to the subjects of his texts, precisely because they are mute things and therefore neutral, is highly personal, subjective, and qualitative: things are given expression, not through a kind of dictation, but by his subjective, textual act, which "takes their side," thereby elevating them to a more dignified status as worthy centers of attention. His poetics constitutes a reversal of the Platonic scheme of things, for the divine source of "inspiration," which alone was truly active according to Plato, has become the completely neutral things of Ponge's work. Therefore, the formerly passive poet is now personally engaged in an original and creative way. Ponge's role as the "voice of mute things" might seem to suggest any number of ideas from pantheism through Baudelaire's "langage des fleurs et des choses muettes" [language of flowers and mute things] ("Elévation," line 20, in Baudelaire 1968), but it is in fact a component of the emphasis that his work puts on process, not product. Indeed, it is not Poetry with a capital P that is valorized. On the contrary, since speech cannot possibly be received from the mute world of things and yet must be used in order to express it, Ponge's writings focus our attention on the very human practice of language, in which he paradoxically locates the salutary presence of the divine *Logos*,[7] which we will continue to discuss in the following chapter.

2
Ponge and the Bible

Just as it is instructive to compare Ponge's understanding of poetry with Plato's, so an examination of the relationship between his work and the Bible can help define his worldview, poetics and ethics. The relationship between Ponge's work and the Bible involves not only allusions to the Scriptures but also the particular way in which they have been arranged on the printed page. For the organization of his published works, Ponge seriously considered using the format of a Protestant Bible that his mother had given to him when he was a boy: on each page, two columns of text, separated by a central column containing references to similar subjects and themes throughout the entire collected works (see *EPS,* 105–6). Such an edition has not been brought out, but the very fact that Ponge imagined it is suggestive. The dream indicates a real desire to preserve the Bible's form, only to replace its metaphysical contents with materialistic texts. Assuming their familiarity with the not uncommon biblical format being used as a model, readers of this edition of Ponge's work would associate it with the Scriptures because both books would share the same distinctive physical arrangement. Ponge would thus appropriate the Bible's prestige in order to undermine its authority more effectively. The form might suggest that a strange sacredness was being conferred on Ponge's poetry, if reflection on its contents did not reveal a parodic slant.

Ponge did not espouse Judeo-Christian theology or theologies in any conventional sense. But, as a poet, he drew from biblical ideas, themes, and images, which constituted an essential part of his cultural heritage. He was born into a Protestant family, to which he refers at several points throughout his writings, and was baptized and raised in the reformed religion, even though, paradoxically, he spent a good part of his youth in the papal city of Avignon (see *PM,* 219–21). This biographical paradox and what he calls the "virtues of the Reformation" (*PM*, 37) help explain not only his role as the champion of Malherbe but also the entire project of philosophical, literary, and ethical reformation that is his work.

This paradox hinges moreover on the author's fierce pride regarding his profoundly Roman (and therefore, according to Ponge, profoundly French) ancestry (see *PM,* 221). On the one hand, his affiliation with ancient Rome is anchored in his relationship to the pre-Christian materialistic poet Lucretius, whom he claims as his principal intellectual forefather. On the other hand, in his poetry as well as in his correspondence with Jean Paulhan, Ponge maintains that he has direct familial ties to a Caesarean legionnaire, and even to the Roman provincial governor Pontius Pilate, who reluctantly authorized Christ's crucifixion (see *PM,* 12, 221; *S,* 106; Paulhan and Ponge 1986, 1:44, 145 n. 1).

Even if historically spurious, this lineage is poetically significant, for it points to Ponge's conscious effort to link himself and his poetry in a most intimate way to the Bible. Owing to this poetic fiction created by Ponge in order to explicate his own work, to read the Bible, in which his forebears play an important role, is to discover and understand his own pre-Christian hereditary values. To refer to the Bible is to reorient it, for these same hereditary values, taken from the Bible itself, become fundaments of his poetry, where they are put into action according to the poet's particular, and often subversive, point of view. They install Ponge's poetry on the Bible's own territory, thereby making his work a worthy adversary.

Ponge was indeed very familiar with the Bible, and his many allusions to it indicate that he admired its literary qualities, while nevertheless feeling compelled to criticize it. As the repository of a metaphysical cosmogony and ethics, and, above all, as the source of the most influential institution promoting this worldview in the society of his day (the Roman Catholic Church), the Bible and its interpretation, for the materialist Ponge, were naturally objects of reflection.

When Ponge alludes to the Bible, he demonstrates his detailed knowledge of the Scriptures, but he also draws our attention to his imaginative interaction with them as material for his poetic creation. In his "Texte sur l'électricité" (Text on electricity), for instance, an entire passage is based on the ark of the covenant built by Moses, and its description in chapter 25 of Exodus:

> [L]'Arche Sainte . . . pourrait être considérée comme un très savant condensateur. Faite, selon les ordres du Seigneur, en bois de sétim (isolant) recouverte sur ses deux faces . . . de feuilles d'or (conductrices), surmontée encore d'une couronne d'or destinée peut-être, grâce au classique "pouvoir des pointes", à provoquer la charge spontanée de l'appareil dans le champ

2 / Ponge and the Bible 39

atmosphérique, lequel, dans ces régions sèches, peut atteindre ... jusqu'à des centaines de volts ... , —il n'est pas étonnant que cette Arche Sainte, toute prête à foudroyer les impies, ait pu être approchée sans danger seulement par les grands prêtres, tels Moïse et Aaron, dont l'Écriture nous apprend par ailleurs qu'ils portaient des vêtements "entièrement tissés de fils d'or et ornés de chaînes d'or traînant jusqu'aux talons". (*GRL*, 156–57)

[The ark of the covenant ... might be understood as a very clever capacitor. Made, following the Lord's instructions, of shittimwood (insulating), covered on both sides ... by gold leaves (conductors), also surmounted by a gold crown intended perhaps, thanks to the classic "property of electrodes," to trigger the spontaneous charging of the apparatus in the atmospheric field, which, in those arid regions can rise ... as high as hundreds of volts ... —it is not surprising that the ark of the covenant, quite ready to subject the impious to a violent electric shock, could have been approached without danger only by the high priests such as Moses or Aaron, about whom the Scriptures tell us moreover that their clothes were "entirely woven with gold threads and decorated with gold chains hanging down to their heels."]

The passage effectively debunks the notion that the powers of the ark might be inexplicable in terms of limited human understanding. These powers are not at all mysterious, since Ponge transforms the ark into a device deriving from scientific study and technological application. If we admire the apparatus, our wonder is not directed toward the almightiness of God, but toward human beings and their scientific understanding and harnessing of nature and its once secret forces, such as electricity. Evoked by the hidden pun on which the text plays as it remotivates the biblical passage, the technological secret of the ark is the discharge of electric particles between electrodes, thereby forming an electric arc.

In chapter 25 of Exodus, God instructs Moses to put golden sculptures of two cherubim facing each other on top of the ark. These cherubim, like gargoyles warding off evil spirits from a church, are to protect the ark from intrusion, and it is between the cherubim that God intends to appear to Moses. Needless to say, the biblical passage makes no mention of electricity. But in the passage by Ponge, the cherubim are replaced with electrodes, and God with electricity: physical powers supplant spiritual powers. If the ark could electrocute the impious who might dare approach it, while sparing Moses and Aaron, this is no miracle: the high priests had simply protected themselves by means of their long robes made of gold—an excellent conductor—which trailed to the earth, thus connecting the electric circuit to a ground. We marvel at their know-how, for, as Ponge puts it, "cette ingénieuse 'mise à la terre' leur permettait de décharger le condensateur sans dommage pour leur personne" [this ingenious "grounding" allowed them to discharge the capacitor without harming themselves] (*GRL*, 157). The text transforms the high priests, who alone have access to the laws of God contained within the ark, into genial scientists, who alone can grasp and exploit the laws of nature. In this light, the "mise à la terre" (grounding) is especially ingenious because it is a metaphor of Ponge's poetics, which connects us with the wonders of the earth and the dynamism of nature.

Some of Ponge's allusions to the Bible are much more explicitly sacrilegious than this. For example, in his "Paroles à propos des nus de Fautrier" (Words about Fautrier's nudes) he first associates the nude with religious architecture, which might already seem shocking, then exclaims:

Non, le véritable scandale, c'est ta cathédrale, ô Jésus!
    Sous les tétons du ciel s'encorbellant aux deux tours, je ne sais quelle étreinte, autour de la rosace du nombril, soude ces dernières, jusqu'à la troublante arcature de la gaine, entre les pilliers.
    Voilà ce que tu laisses voir du parvis, Notre-Dame de Paris, tandis que vers ton abside, cambrée comme les reins d'une chatte, les mariniers d'amont, à mains pleines, guindent leur timon. (*GRL*, 119)

[No, the real scandal is your cathedral, o Jesus!
    Under the breasts of the sky, like corbels against the two towers, I don't know what kind of embrace, around the rose window of the navel, binds the towers together, right up to the arousing arcaded girdle, between the pillars.
    That is what you allow one to see from the square in front of you, Notre Dame of Paris, while toward your apse, arched like the loins of a cat in heat, the upstream sailors, with hands full, make their tiller stiff.]

Parts of the human body are assimilated to the architectural elements of the cathedral, which were intended to symbolize the immaterial purity of God. The cathedral consecrated to the Virgin Mary is imagined as an enticing woman in her undergarments—"la troublante arcature de la gaine" [the arousing arcaded girdle]—having orgiastic sexual relations with eager (upstream) sailors who paw and prepare to penetrate her as she lasciviously arches her back (upstream on the Seine is indeed behind the cathedral).

This conflation is further encouraged by the overlapping meanings of the word *rein(s)*, which, in addition to its anatomical sense (i.e., loins), also designates the lower, rising part of a vault, such as the cathedral's apse. It thereby completes the picture of the Cathedral-Virgin raising her hindquarters like a cat in heat ("ton abside, cambrée comme les reins d'une chatte"). A scandalous scene indeed, because it ridicules the doctrine of the virgin birth as it poetically remotivates the etymology of *cathédrale*. An implicit pun on *chaire/chair* (pulpit/flesh)—the Latin *cathedra* (denoting *chaire* [pulpit] in French) being the root of *cathédrale*—evokes the opposition between the pulpit and the flesh, between spirituality and carnality. Mary is redefined as a sexual being, and thus the passage insists on the sensual origin of Jesus, emphasizing his humanness to the detriment of his divinity.

That Ponge thought of and presented his work as a type of sacred book is also illustrated by passages such as the following, from his text "La Seine" (The Seine). After describing the origin of life on earth from a scientific point of view, Ponge writes: "Voilà donc, cher ami, comment notre imagination nous permet de décrire ce que les précédents livres sacrés nommèrent la Genèse" [So that is, dear friend, how our imagination allows us to describe what the previous sacred books called Genesis] (*TP*, 596). From Ponge's point of view, there are precursors in the genre of the sacred book—a blasphemous opinion, from the perspective of Christian dogma, for it implies that Christianity is not the only true religion. And he intends to inscribe his work within this tradition by bringing a different angle to bear on its subject matter and the way in which it is treated. If he feels the need to rewrite the account of creation in Genesis, it is because he believes that the topic is of great significance, but that another approach to it is worthier.

Details regarding Ponge's place within the tradition of what he considers to be sacred books, as well as further supplanting of biblical authority in this domain, are provided in the same text by references to the godlike Epicurus, whose teachings could hardly be more opposed to the Bible's: "Nous trouverions aisément leçon de tout cela dans l'immortel Epicure" [We would easily find a lesson concerning all that in the immortal Epicurus] (*TP*, 548). Ponge extols Epicurus in such a way as to recall Lucretius's own praise of him. Not only does this treatment of Epicurus as a near god and savior of humanity remind us of the same in *De rerum natura*, but the didactic style of Lucretius's materialistic poem is echoed here. Just as Lucretius was attempting to turn the aristocratic politician Memmius from mythological to Epicurean explanations of the world, so, with a similar ethical goal in mind, Ponge is trying to convert the reader, whom he addresses by the ingratiating "mon ami" [my friend]. For him, this is a sacred endeavor.

From this point of view, Ponge's work is an apostolic act, and his text ironically mixes Christian and Epicurean discipleship by means of the homophonic pun of the title: the Last Supper (*la Cène* in French), during which Christ instituted the Eucharist, is at once evoked and replaced by

"La Seine" [the river Seine]. Indeed, Ponge's strategy presents a structure that is similar to that of a homophone: his expression may sometimes sound Christian, but its origin and meaning are in fact quite different. An analogical connection between Ponge's work and Christianity is established in his writings; the analogy, however, reveals not only a similarity but, what is more important, a difference. It is not communion with the spirit of God in which Ponge finds the source of his poetry, but in the real waters of the Seine, "ces flots de l'inspiration" [these waves of inspiration] (526).

In Ponge's text, it is not Christianity, but French civilization that is disseminated throughout the world thanks to the Seine. The diverse elements of the world, not just the body of Christians, are brought together as in communion by the river, because they all eventually participate in the civilization that it nourishes. As it crosses through France, it also crosses all occupational, national, cultural, and racial boundaries: the river Seine "appartient au géographe, à son concierge, à l'historien, au marinier, au pêcheur, au poète, à tout Français, au touriste, au philosophe — à l'écolier, qu'il soit blanc ou noir, aussi" [belongs to the geographer, his or her caretaker, the historian, the sailor, the poet, each French person, the tourist, the philosopher—the pupil too, whether white or black] (528). We are all one in the Seine, just as through the ritualized version of *la Cène* we all commune with God.

"La Seine" evokes the symbolic ingestion of Christ's blood and body, thereby proposing it as an implicit analogy. But the analogy emphasizes the more material nutrition with which the river has always blessed France, "cette civilisation très ancienne qui s'abreuve et fleurit précisément sur ces bords" [this very ancient civilization that drinks and blossoms right on its banks] (526). "La Seine" would seem to reflect the essence of France as the elements of the Eucharist symbolize the essence of Christ. Ponge's celebration of the Seine would therefore be to French literature what the ritualized version of *la Cène* is to the Church.

But the text is opposed to the Roman Catholic version of the sacrament because Ponge's writings are based on the ancient materialistic analogy between the elements of the text and those of the external world. "La Seine" is, as Ponge puts it, considering the liquid state of matter constituting the river Seine, a *"discours liquide fluent" [fluent liquid discourse]* (542): the text is stylistically conformable to the reality of its subject. It is an analogical presentation, not a symbolic representation of the qualities of the thing to which it refers. The Roman Catholic doctrine of transubstantiation, on the other hand, maintains that, upon consecration, the substances of the bread and the wine are changed into the body and blood of Jesus Christ. After consecration, only nonessential qualities, or accidents, of the bread and the wine remain, such as their appearance. This magical aspect of the sacraments, against which the Reformation rebelled, finds no echo in the analogy connecting Ponge's work and Christianity. Although the goal of Ponge's poetics is to bring these separate realities as close together as possible through the textual act, the two "worlds"—the world of language and the external world—are admittedly separate and distinct:

> Quand je dis que nous devons utiliser ce monde des mots, pour exprimer notre sensibilité au monde extérieur, je pense, je ne sais pas si j'ai tort, et c'est en ça je crois que je ne suis pas mystique, en tous cas je pense que ces deux mondes sont étanches, c'est-à-dire sans passage de l'un à l'autre. ("La Pratique de la littérature," in *GRM*, 275–76)

> [When I say that we must use this world of words in order to express our sensitivity to the external world, I think, I don't know whether I'm wrong, and it is in this regard that I believe I'm not a mystic, in any case I think these two worlds are watertight, that is, there is no passageway from one to the other.]

There is no "transubstantiation" of language into phenomena of the external world.

Ponge's predilection for analogies that at once link and differentiate between Christianity, Epicurean materialism, and French civilization surfaces in other texts. In his *Pour un Malherbe*, for instance, Malherbe is compared to a Father of the Church, but it is the church of French letters: "Dans ce donné français, Malherbe occupe la place d'un *Père*, comme on dit des Pères de l'Eglise" [In this French element, Malherbe occupies the place of a *Father*, as one says of the Fathers of the Church] (*PM*, 57). Through Malherbe, God, Lucretius, and Epicurus intersect paradoxically, as we learn from one of the author's friends:

> Since I did not possess a copy of his *Nouveau Recueil*, Francis Ponge inscribed one to me the day before the presentation of the 1974 *Books Abroad*/Neustadt International Prize for literature.[1] Part of the inscription reads as follows: "On this *13th* day of June in Norman [location of the University of Oklahoma] I very happily inscribe this book, which I brought especially for [Ivar Ivask] from the Mas des Vergers [Ponge's house in the south of France], while we live in a bizarre fashion awaiting the decision of the wind which, for better or worse, will shift a rather dangerous cloud . . . ! But the *sapientia* of Lucretius—which he inherited from Epicurus—keeps us serene, or as Malherbe was later to formulate: 'To desire that which God wants is the only way of maintaining our serenity.'" . . . The cloud was real, . . . consisting of phosphorous trichloride.

... There had been a major train derailment on the morning of the 13th outside Moore. Several canisters containing this gas had been punctured. ... (Ivask 1974, 647; translations from French by Ivask)

Ponge states that his book is founded on Malherbe's work understood as an important historical act, and he considers the word *act* in the sense of the Acts of the Apostles (*PM*, 299). In the same work, however, Ponge interprets Malherbe's position in the development of French literature as being intermediate between that of Lucretius and his own (262, 282). Malherbe is therefore an apostle of a materialistic poetic tradition that has its roots in *De rerum natura*. Following this subversive analogy, Lucretius is like Christ, and Epicurus like God, for the Roman poet expressed the Greek philosopher's thought, thereby making it available to a larger part of the world. If Malherbe is comparable to a father of the church because through his work the tradition of poetic materialism has been transferred to the French language, Ponge's work, as it continues this tradition, which is philosophically opposed to biblical metaphysics, is comparable to a kind of contemporary anti-Church.

This church of French literature is a reformed church, since Ponge carries forth the apostleship of Malherbe, who, according to Ponge, embodies the qualities of the Reformation: "Malherbe, en un sens, c'était les vertus de la Réforme (je sais, il n'en était pas, mais tout comme)" [Malherbe, in a way, embodied the virtues of the Reformation (I know, he wasn't a part of it, but it is as though he had been)] (*PM*, 37). By reference to the Reformation, Ponge gives analogical depth to Malherbe's rupture with the poetics of the Pléiade. Malherbe's reform is understood as the literary equivalent of Protestantism, with which it is historically intertwined. The Pléiade, following the underlying analogy, is therefore like Catholicism. Malherbe's rupture with the Pléiade—his rejection of its frequent mythological allusions, its poetic abandon, its Latinate language so far removed from actual usage—contributed to a more modern point of view according to which poetry is above all craft, not inspiration or magic, and the poem is produced by salutary creative constraints.[2]

Ponge's work develops the discourse of a parodic countermagic. For example, throughout his writings it is implied that his particular treatment of things gives a voice to them. Phenomena of the external world—the "mute world of things"—would acquire speech thanks to the transmutation accomplished by Ponge's alchemical art: lowly things would be transformed into the subjects of the elevated domain of poetry. They would obtain the ability to elate our mind and spirit. This ironic magic draws our attention away from the idea-centered literature against which Ponge reacts in order to refocus our attention on the neglected things of our daily life. Ponge's art offers us an amazing voyage inside things, and thereby introduces us to their heretofore unexplored poetic potential, as in this passage where the praises of soap are sung:

> Eh: Oui! A rien ne sert de vivre sous la pompe. Ni voire de séjourner dans l'eau du Jourdain. (Il vaut bien mieux la plus simple cuvette . . .) Si l'on ne tient en mains (si l'on n'emploie) ce médiocre galet (de nature magique) . . . et si on ne lui donne la parole.
> A peine l'a-t-on sollicité, quelle éloquence! (*S*, 32–33)
>
> [Hey: Yes! Living under the pump is useless. Or even staying in the waters of the Jordan. (The simplest washbowl would be far better . . .) If one doesn't hold in one's hands (if one doesn't use) this ordinary pebble (of magical nature) . . . and if one doesn't give it speech.
> One has hardly appealed to it, what eloquence!]

Once initiated into Ponge's particular concept of poetry, we experience the purifying effect of a new kind of baptism, which miraculously washes away the pomp of Poetry with a capital *P*. By means of subversive allusions to the Bible, his poetry replaces the spiritual with the physical (the river Jordan where Jesus was baptized being replaced with the simplest washbasin). And, in order to appreciate this materialism with rejuvenated eyes, we are invited into Ponge's anti-Church, where we will participate in a reformed sacrament of baptism, a kind of "toilette intellectuelle" [intellectual hygiene] (*S*, 29, 32).

Similar to Ponge's "toilette intellectuelle," Malherbe's "désaffublement de la poésie" [ridding poetry of bizarre and ridiculous trappings] (*PM*, 96), which is so very much to Ponge's liking, is integrated into the analogy between Protestantism's movement away from what Ponge perceives as the ritualized trappings and magical aspects of Catholicism, and the way in which his work directs our attention away from "la Poésie" (Poetry) while refocusing it on "la Parole" [the Word] (78). Malherbe's work, as it reinforces his own, constitutes a literary sacrament for Ponge, as may be seen in the following passage, where, irritated by Guez de Balzac's criticism of Malherbe, Ponge finds and rereads an incriminated stanza: "La voici. . . . Sans doute y allions-nous un peu comme au sacrifice, ou plutôt à la *communion*. Nous ne nous attendions pas cependant à y trouver une justification si éblouissante, un vrai soleil de Saint-Sacrement!" [Here it is. . . . We were probably approaching it somewhat as though we were going to a sacrifice, or rather to *Communion*. We hadn't, however, expected to find such a dazzling justification in it, a real Blessed Sacrament sun!] (277–78).

For Ponge, speech, skillfully arranged in Malherbe's "concert de vocables" or in his own work, is divine because, like the Christ of the Incarnation, the Word is a mixture of matter and spirit: "O Divinité, notre seule raison d'être, ô Parole, matière et esprit mêlés" [O Divinity, our only justification for existing, o Speech, matter and spirit mingled] ("Nous, mots français: Essai de prose civique," in *NNR,* 102). According to this understanding of poetic language, however, the *logos* is not an objective presence, appearing in a particular place or in a specific form. This view therefore constitutes a movement away from the Christian notion of the *Logos* as a concrete reality, as the absolute and unique incarnation of God in the historical man, Jesus Christ. Rather, it is much closer to the Greek philosophical *logos*, which was understood as a universal principle. For Ponge, then, *logos* refers to the meaningful structure of reality that manifests itself any number of times in any number of forms.[3]

Although Ponge did not understand the Word (*le Verbe*) in a biblical sense, there is nonetheless an analogical connection to this aspect of Judeo-Christian theology, for his writings appropriate the biblical metaphor of God as author. In biblical cosmogony, it is the Word that is considered to be the creative principle underlying all material and spiritual reality, and Christ the savior was the Word incarnate. The analogy functions in such a way as to bring Ponge's linguistic materialism into relief by contrasting it with a metaphysical notion of the word and the world, especially since the poet specifies that this parallel is relevant only as an analogy:

> [J]e suis entré dans la familiarité des bois de pins.... [Ils] ont acquis leur chance de sortir du monde muet... pour entrer dans celui de la parole, de l'utilisation par l'homme à ses fins morales, enfin dans le Logos, ou, si l'on préfère et pour parler par analogie, dans le Royaume de Dieu. ("Le Carnet du bois de pins," in *TP,* 339)

> [I entered into the familiarity of the pine woods.... They have won their chance to come out of the mute world ... so as to enter that of the word, of use by humans with their ethical ends in view, in short, enter the Logos, or, if one prefers and to speak analogically, the Kingdom of God.]

According to this passage, thanks to the creative power of his words, Ponge has given linguistic life to the pine forest, and the text becomes a kind of paradise (or Kingdom of God) for its readers as well as for the pine forest itself.

The notion of bringing things and readers together in a kind of literary paradise appears also in Ponge's *Le Savon* (Soap). In this text, Ponge refers to his work as a "nouvelle Écriture" [new Scripture] (118). The capital E implies a kind of new Bible where the act of writing itself proffers the *logos*, and whose goal is to reveal the relative moral lessons contained within the plurality of things, and not the absolute truth of a single manifestation of the *Logos*. Indeed, he calls his work a bible, but by manipulating the material aspect of the word—changing its gender from feminine to masculine—he indicates the philosophical difference between his bible and the Bible: "Et voilà le pourquoi des *choses* (et par exemple du savon) dans mon livre, ma bible (dans *mon* bible, ai-je envie d'écrire)" [And that is the reason for *things* (and for example soap) in my book, my bible [feminine, as is standard in French] (in *my* bible [masculine adjective used], I feel like writing)] (118). Once again, his writings are presented as though they were Holy Writ, for the reader's conflation of them and the Bible is encouraged in the passage by the humorous fusion of separate words of different genders into a single word referring to Ponge's work: *mon livre* and *ma bible* are compacted into *mon bible*.

Owing to its remarkably agrammatical character, this name given to his work attracts our attention to an important aspect of Ponge's project: the act of naming as creative act.[4] The act of naming, for Ponge, also involves writing; for him, naming entails marking. This distinction is important because the act of marking mediates between different aspects of language: the visible, written word recalls the sonority of the invisible, spoken word, and thereby adds body to language. As Ponge often insists, words are just such bodies. Indeed, his use of them is conditioned by the fact that he considers them to be "three-dimensional": a dimension for the ear, another for the eye, and a metaphorical third dimension that is their meaning (see *GRM,* 272–73). Ponge's notion of the word as a body allows for the "resurrection" of words and the alphabetical elements from which they are made: they are physical things buried in the dictionary, where the associative networks they contain and have contained are conserved.

One of the manifestations of this poetic process in Ponge's writings may be observed in his text *Comment une figue de paroles et pourquoi* (How a fig of words and why).[5] In this work, which includes several biblical allusions, the author's signature appears frequently. He signs, naming himself "Franciscus Pontius," which modifies his real name and, at the same time, introduces it into a seemingly foreign set of associations where it functions analogically. *Pontius* reminds us of the Latin *pons- pontis* (bridge), the proper noun Pontius Pilate (whom Ponge has claimed as an ancestor), and, indirectly, of Christ, owing to Pilate's role in the Crucifixion.

Ponge was not obligated, but rather chose, to modify the spelling of his name: there is no grammatical rule that would have prevented him from transforming Ponge into the Latin Pongius. But instead of the *g* we might expect, we find the letter *t*. This incongruity encourages us to explore something so small as to seem almost unworthy of notice, that is, the letter *t*; but examining such elementary phenomena and their virtual significance is appropriate in the context of Ponge's linguistic materialism, which constantly focuses on the lowly things that we tend to find unworthy of our admiration.

A learned modern reader might perceive a hidden sense within the *t* of Pontius. The letter *t* in modern European languages using the Latin alphabet derives from the last sign of the Phoenician alphabet, which had the consonantal value *t*, and appeared in these interchangeable, cruciform variations: + and x. The name given to this sign, *taw*, means "mark." Of all the letters of this seminal, ancient alphabet, only *taw* designates not a phenomenon of the natural world, but a human activity: designating by a mark, and therefore naming. By replacing the *g* of Ponge with the *t* of Pontius, Ponge has therefore not only evoked the name Pontius Pilate but he has also put naming as such at the center of his signature.

Indeed, the naming act itself associates the author with Pilate as a major participant in the story of the Crucifixion, for the act of naming is central to the relationship between Pilate and Jesus, as recounted in the Scriptures. According to all four Gospels, before putting Jesus to death, the governor "named" him: "Pilate therefore said unto him, Art thou a king then? Jesus answered, Thou sayest that I am a king" (John 18:37). Against the will of those who were persecuting Jesus, Pilate's name for him—"King of the Jews"—was subsequently marked on the cross for all to see, thereby elevating him through language from the lowly status of a common criminal to that of an exalted ruler (see John 19:19–22).

It is this aspect of Pilate's role that Ponge is considering when, in *Le Savon*, he exonerates his supposed ancestor, washing away the common perception of him as a dirty scoundrel:

> [I]l ne s'agit que du savon et de se laver les mains, à l'instar de mon ancêtre Ponce Pilate — dont je suis si fier qu'après avoir dit: "Qu'est-ce que la vérité?" — il se soit lavé les mains de la mort du Juste (ou de l'exalté) et soit ainsi le seul personnage du conte à être entré dans l'histoire les mains pures, ayant fait son devoir sans grands gestes, grands symboles, vagissements et fatuité. (*S*, 106)

> [It's only about soap and washing one's hands, following the example of my ancestor Pontius Pilate—of whom I am so proud that after having said: "What is truth?"—he should have washed his hands of the death of

the Just One (or the exalted one) and thus be the only character in the tale to have entered into history with pure hands, having done his duty without big gestures, big symbols, cries, and self-complacency.]

Ponge offers Pilate's role in the story of the Crucifixion as an analogy of his own actions in relation to the subjects of his poetry. As Jesus' persecutors saw him in an unfavorable light, so many readers may find common objects, such as a fig or a piece of soap, undeserving of poetic presentation. But Ponge sees no fault in these things, and, on the contrary, praises them in his poetry, just as Pilate, after speaking to the derided Jesus, found no fault in him, and, indeed, exalted him by having "King of the Jews" displayed on the cross.

Things, and the way in which they are explored poetically by Ponge, are a means of introducing the reader into a kind of paradise. This paradise is the moral goal of his poetics of the *objoie*, which emphasizes the textual structure as joyously signifying itself: "Quand au paradis de ce livre, qu'est-ce donc? Qu'est-ce que cela pouvait être, sinon, lecteur, *ta lecture* (comme elle mord sa queue en ces dernières lignes)" [As for the paradise of this book, what is it then? What could it be, if not, reader, *your reading* (as it bites its tail in these last lines)] (*S*, 128). This passage—from the last page of *Le Savon*—may evoke ancient pagan symbols of divine completion, such as the Ouroboros (the snake that bites its own tail); but in the context of Ponge's biblical analogies and his linguistic materialism, it also inescapably reminds us of one of the Scriptures' own metaphors—from the last book of the Bible—which links the self-contained, eternal perfection of God to the alphabetical letters, elements of all linguistic phenomena: "I am Alpha and Omega, the beginning and the ending" (Rev. 1:8). Ponge appropriates the notion of the self-sufficient, eternal perfection of God, only to remotivate it poetically in order to make it express an opposing, materialistic vision of the means and end of creation. The last sentence of the text makes this clear, for it insists on the reader's sensory perception of material elements, from which all meaning derives: "Son sort [celui du livre] ne dépend plus que de la nature matérielle dont ces signes et leur support font partie" [Its fate {that of the book} no longer depends on anything other than the material nature of which these signs and their physical medium are parts] (*S,* 128). In this way, Ponge affirms that, concerning his work as a bible, there is no creation ex nihilo, and thus contradicts the Old Testament account of creation, where this doctrine is implicit.

As the concept of creation out of nothing was essential for the historical differentiation between paganism and monotheism, and thus for the establishment of the early Church, Ponge's subversion of it brings his relationship to the Bible full circle and provides yet another bridge to his ancestral principles. Through Lucretius's poetic analogy between atoms and letters, Ponge's poetics is anchored in the cosmogony of Epicurus, according to which nothing is created out of nothing. Everything, even mind or spirit—and the spirit of the text—is the result of the arrangement of the same elements, and therefore of a natural process of repetition and recreation.

In expressing this notion, the end of *Le Savon* is linked to its beginning. Throughout the text, the reader confronts an unusually high number of repetitions—the same physical elements reappear frequently and in so doing mimic the repeated "paroles" of soap. This formal imitation emphasizes *Le Savon* as a textually adequate analogue of its subject: soap's "continuel don de salive" [continual gift of saliva] (127), its ceaseless lather, is recreated by the repetitive nature of the text, as in this repetitive early passage:

> Mais d'abord, que je vous prévienne!
>
> Vous serez étonnés, peut-être — car ce n'est pas très habituel en matière littéraire — des fréquentes, des fastidieuses répétitions que comporte le présent texte.
>
> Très souvent vous remarquerez: "Mais il se répète! Mais j'ai déjà entendu cela, il y a à peine quelques minutes!"
>
> Eh bien, dois-je m'en excuser? Non! Je n'aime pas beaucoup m'excuser, et puis, après tout, ces façons, ces manières que vous admettez fort bien, n'est-ce pas, en matière de musique: ces répétitions, ces reprises *da capo*, ces variations sur un même thème, ces compositions en forme de fugue que vous admettez fort bien en musique, que vous admettez et dont vous jouissez — pourquoi nous seraient-elles, en matière de littérature, interdites?
>
> Pouvez-vous me le dire?
>
> En tout cas, vous voici prévenus.
>
> C'est ainsi, après tout, que je travaille, c'est ainsi que naissent en moi les développements, c'est ainsi que l'esprit progresse, — et il faut bien, n'est-ce pas? être honnête, il faut bien ne pas tricher avec le mouvement de l'esprit? (12–13)

> [But first, let me warn you!
>
> You will be surprised, perhaps—for it isn't very common where literature is concerned—by the frequent, the fastidious repetitions of which the present text is composed.
>
> Very often you will observe: "But he repeats himself! But I've already heard that, scarcely a few minutes ago!"
>
> Well, must I apologize for this? No! I don't much like to apologize, and then, after all, these ways and manners which you accept willingly,

isn't it so, as regards music: these repetitions, these reprises *da capo*, these variations on the same theme, these compositions in the form of a fugue that you accept happily in music, that you accept and enjoy—why should they, where literature is concerned, be forbidden?
Can you tell me?
In any case, now you've been warned.
This is the way, after all, that I work, this is the way that developments happen in me, this is the way that the mind progresses—and one must definitely, mustn't one? be honest, one must definitely not play tricks with the movement of the mind?]

As Ponge's work carries on a critical dialogue with Plato as a representative of ancient idealism in order to support a materialistic vision, it also develops a relationship with the Bible for a similar reason. Ponge's productive confrontation with the Bible is part of a larger strategy involving the poetic appropriation and remotivation of opposing worldviews. His writings convert the Bible to materialism by rereading its metaphysical explanations in scientific and sensual contexts. His poetic analogies assimilate the development of French civilization to that of Christianity, and suggest that his role in the French poetic church is founded ultimately on Epicurean materialism, which, as embodied by Lucretius, and as carried forth by Ponge, is at the center of the salvation and paradise that his work proposes.

Ponge's iconoclasm is not confined to literary debates alone: the above passage, for instance, offers the art of musical composition as a theoretical model for Ponge's poetic materialism. It is a surprising analogy, given that we tend to think of music—unlike the plastic arts—as the preeminently immaterial art. The next chapter will therefore explore the relationship between Ponge's work and music in the context of an interartistic version of his subversive values.

3
Ponge and Rameau

> La plus basse corde... [qui] vibre à la limite de la musique, du son pur, et du silence [The lowest string... vibrating at the limits of music, of pure sound, and of silence].
> —Ponge, "Faune et flore"

The writings of Francis Ponge are often associated with the visual arts. His book entitled *L'Atelier contemporain* (The contemporary workshop) justifies this link, since it is comprised of laudatory essays on artists such as Picasso and Braque, the sculptor Giacometti, and others, many of whom were Ponge's friends. But even when he speaks of these artists, comparisons are sometimes made with music, as in this passage on the art of Jean Fautrier, where Ponge's comment fuses painting and music: "Chaque tronçon de son oeuvre sonn[e] comme la peinture entière, comme la lyre elle-même" [Every section of his work resonates as does painting as a whole, as does the lyre itself] ("Fautrier, d'un seul bloc fougueusement équarri," in *AC*, 144).

The art of music was indeed of great significance to Ponge. In his *Pour un Malherbe*, which many consider to be his *ars poetica*, Ponge reveals that during his youth he passionately studied music, his instrument being the piano, and that his musical education was to no negligible extent encouraged by his mother and father, who were themselves musicians (*PM*, 209). Moreover, in the same work he states that the primary artistic values and principles that he retained from his formative years were musical ones (209).[1]

But Ponge's many allusions to musicians from Bach to Stravinsky have not been sufficiently explored. Indeed, the number of times Ponge refers to the French composer Rameau is especially striking: he wrote an essay on him, and he referred to him many times throughout his entire work. The question is how does Ponge make use of the link to music, the most immaterial of the arts (according to a persistent nineteenth-century conviction), in support of his well-known materialistic, even Epicurean worldview. I would first like to examine the relationship between Ponge, Rameau, and music on a theoretical level, and afterwards illustrate its resonance in Ponge's poetry.

Jean-Philippe Rameau, in his *Traité de l'harmonie réduite à ses principes naturels* (Treatise on harmony reduced to its natural principles), and in a characteristically eighteenth-century effort to anchor his principle of harmonic generation in nature, relates the function of what he calls the "fundamental bass" by appropriating an analogy advanced by the theorist Zarlino, whom he quotes:

> "De même que la terre sert de fondement aux autres éléments, de même aussi la basse a la propriété de soutenir, d'établir et de fortifier les autres parties; de sorte qu'elle est prise pour la base et pour le fondement de l'harmonie, d'où elle est appelée basse, comme qui dirait la base et le soutien." Et après avoir supposé que si la terre venait à manquer, tout ce bel ordre de la nature tomberait en ruine, il dit, "pareillement si la basse venait à manquer, toute la pièce de musique serait remplie de dissonances et de confusion."[2]

> ["As the earth is the foundation for the other elements, just so the role of the bass is to sustain, establish, and strengthen the other parts. Therefore it is understood to be the basis and foundation of harmony and is called the bass—the basis and support, as it were." After supposing that, if the earth were to disappear, all the beautiful order of nature would collapse into ruin, he says that "in like manner, if the bass were to disappear, the entire musical composition would be full of dissonance and confusion."]

Surprisingly, and perhaps paradoxically, despite the centuries that separate them and regardless of the differences between their arts, Francis Ponge, in his book significantly entitled *Méthodes* (Methods), declares:

> J.-Ph. Rameau est l'artiste au monde qui m'intéresse le plus profondément. Je n'en finirais plus . . . si je voulais marquer point par point les éléments (de profonde similitude) qui font de lui . . . mon parent. . . . Toutes ses articulations harmoniques . . . naissent à partir de la grave musicalité d'une basse fondamentale exprimant l'épaisseur et le fonctionnement en profondeur du monde. La mélodie, chez lui, n'est jamais que le profil ou comme la silhouette de l'harmonie: sa musique a trois dimensions. . . . D'où lui viennent-elles, [ses vertus]? De ce qu'il vit enfermé dans son langage. ("La Société du génie," in *GRM*, 207, 211–12)

[J.-Ph. Rameau is, of all the artists in the world, the one who interests me the most deeply. It would take forever ... if I wanted to indicate point by point the elements (of deep similarity) that make him ... my relative. ... All his harmonic articulations ... arise from the low musicality of a fundamental bass expressing the thickness and the in-depth functioning of the world. Melody, in his work, is always just the profile or like the silhouette of harmony: where do his virtues come from? From the fact that he lives within the confines of his language.]

And he continues, advancing notions that are sure to disconcert linguists:

Or, qu'est-ce qu'un langage, sinon un univers, mais fini. Comme [Rameau] est aussi très sensible à la nature—elle, un univers infini—cela l'amène d'une part à adopter une théorie matérialisant la nature (afin d'en faire un univers fini), d'autre part à articuler vers l'infini son langage, afin de rapprocher autant que possible ces deux mondes. (212)

[Now, what is a language, if not a universe, but finite. As Rameau is also very sensitive to nature—it being an infinite universe—this leads him, on the one hand, to adopt a theory that materializes nature (in order to make a finite universe of it), and, on the other hand, to articulate his language toward the infinite, in order to bring these two worlds as close together as possible.]

Ponge's perception of Rameau's harmonic theories, as related in this passage, presents a remarkable insistence on the semes of "verticality" and "depth," with its repetition of the associated words *profondément* (deeply), *profonde* (deep), *grave* (low, and also deep), *basse fondamentale* (fundamental, i.e., lowest or deepest bass), *épaisseur* (thickness or depth), and *profondeur* (depth). This semantic insistence is furthermore brought into relief thanks to the contrasting semes of "linearity" and "superficiality," which are related by the figurative presentation of melody as a profile or silhouette. This contrast is Ponge's way of distinguishing between melodic and harmonic aspects of music. Melody, according to the passage, is thin, like a profile or silhouette turned onto its side, since its separately sounded single notes unfold linearly, sequentially over time, in the horizontal direction of musical writing. Harmony, on the other hand, provides a full body for the silhouette of melody, in that at any given moment in time, and in the vertical dimension of the musical score, a relatively dense plurality of tones is heard simultaneously. In this way, Rameau's music is, as Ponge says, three-dimensional; that is, the two-dimensional melodic profile is rendered three-dimensional by the accompanying flesh and bones of harmony. It is interesting to note that, as one might expect, relatively more importance is given, in the passage, to terms relating to harmony than to those having to do with melody: six terms evoking the thickness of harmony as opposed to only two suggesting the thinness of the melodic line. This is a revealing example of the way in which Ponge's poetry mimes its subject. Here, the subject of the text is Rameau's own insistence on the greater importance of harmony; as Rameau's well-known declaration would have it: "C'est l'harmonie qui nous guide" [It is harmony that guides us]. In this way, Ponge's text underscores points of contact between Rameau's understanding of musical language and his own views concerning language and poetry.

According to Ponge's metapoetic notion of "épaisseur sémantique" [semantic depth, thickness, and density] the poet is to expose and exploit simultaneously—like the musician who exploits various harmonic articulations—the entire semantic range of words as contained in the historical-etymological dictionary, the Littré dictionary to be precise.[3] This dictionary is conceived of as a self-contained universe. Ponge's desire to reduce language to its semantic dimension alone is, according to our reading of his comments on Rameau, modeled on the musician's craft as it derives from his codification of functional harmony, since Ponge calls Rameau "mon parent" [my relative]. Rameau's fundamental bass and the tones of his harmonies, which are aligned vertically in time and thus sounded simultaneously, are likened to the inclusion or evocation of the etymological root and its various semantic overtones, which are arranged in Ponge's text following his principle of the poetic exploitation of language's "épaisseur sémantique."[4] This vertical alignment of harmonic or semantic associations is, then, according to both Rameau and Ponge, the most important artistic concern.

Ponge's use of music in his poetic compositions, as well as what may be called his notion of "paradigmatic poetry" or "textual harmony," is illustrated strikingly by his text "L'Araignée" (The spider) (*GRP*, 127-31).[5] The poem is explicitly structured along musical lines, as its sections correspond to the different dance pieces that are woven into the baroque form known as the suite, as practiced by such composers as Bach and Rameau. This very structure helps construct the spider's "métaphore tissée" [woven metaphor]. It also justifies the text's many puns and metaphors and, in general, its extremely "baroque" exploitation of the phonetic or musical qualities of language.

The poem begins by an "argument" in the form of an epigraph, which is an abstract of the text's narrative progression:

EXORDE EN COURANTE / PROPOSITION (THEME DE LA SARABANDE). / COURANTE EN SENS INVERSE (CONFIRMATION). / SARABANDE, LA TOILE OURDIE / (GIGUE D'INSECTS VOLANT AUTOUR). / FUGUE EN CONCLUSION.[6]

[EXORDIUM IN THE FORM OF A COURANTE {with the punning overtones of "exordium while running" (phonetically similar to *en courant*) and "with the runs" *(la courante)*, since the spider is running while secreting/excreting its web}. / PROPOSITION (THEME OF THE SARABAND). / REVERSED COURANTE {with the overtone of "running in the opposite direction"} (CONFIRMATION). / SARABAND {with the punning overtone of "it tautens again" (phonetically similar to *ça rebande*)}, THE WEB WOVEN / (GIGUE OF INSECTS FLYING AROUND). / FUGUE IN CONCLUSION.][7]

The text's musical microstructure proposes an interpretive strategy.[8]

The first part of the argument is striking because it combines terms from the realms of discourse ("exorde") and music ("courante"). This mixture constitutes the first of the poem's many formal imitations of conflation as such, which is one of the text's principle themes. "Exorde" signifies the beginning of a prose sermon, while "courante" means a seventeenth-century French dance composed of running and gliding steps in triple time. The word *courante* derives from *courir*, to run, and is therefore a fitting partial description/definition of the spider, since it refers to its initial activity, its "exordium": the running and gliding of the arachnean dancer as it secretes "le fil de son discours" [the thread of its discourse], thus laying the framework of its web (or metaphorical text).

In the second line of the argument, the formal imitation of conflation is continued by the unusual combination of rhetorical and musical terms within the unit of the phrase. Both "proposition" and "thème" ("thème de la sarabande") signify the putting forth of a plan, but these words come from different areas of activity, rhetoric and music, respectively. Since these activities are exclusively human, and yet associated here with the spider, the metaphorical relationship between spider and poet is reinforced.

The contrast of rhythms between the rapid courante and the slow and stately saraband suggests a change in the spider's activity. Whereas the courante summons up the rapid weaving of the web, or the lines of the text as they are "secreted" by the author's pen, the saraband suggests the spider's relative immobility as it awaits the arrival of its preys on the completed web—"sarabande, la toile ourdie" [saraband, the web woven]—or the poet who expects critical glosses, like insects, to get stuck to the text/web.

A further rhythmic contrast—between "sarabande" and "gigue"—is introduced in the argument, and another moment in the narrative is thereby suggested: the insects flying around the web. The particularly lively pace of the gigue, with its rhythmic long-short effect, is well suited to the evocation of the jittery, uneven flight of small insects approaching the web.

In like manner, each section of the poem proper corresponds to a dance movement of the musical suite delineated in the argument: various formal imitations of the dances' characteristic rhythms inform the description of the spider's (or prey's) activities. For instance, the rhythmic alternation between the rapid courante and the slower saraband is rendered by a typographical difference between the first and second sections of the poem: the second section is composed exclusively of blocked, capital letters, which appear rather static after the "normal" characters of the first section. This striking change in typographical characters suggests a corresponding rhythmical modification in the spider's movements. The long list that constitutes the poem's fifth section is another good example; its subject being the "gigue d'insectes volant autour [de la toile]" [gigue of insects flying around {the web}], this section is appropriately (and humorously) printed in "pattes de mouche" (literally, fly's feet, but also meaning a spidery scrawl). The repetitive, limping rhythm of the gigue is further suggested by the alternation between the short lines of two, then three, elements: "doctes et bavardins, / badins, taquins, mutins" [scholars and chatterers, / pranksters, teasers, mutineers], etc.

The poem's final section ("fugue en conclusion") continues the narrative of the spider's activity in its concluding phase, and evokes it by a phonetic rendition of the musical form of the fugue. The first word of the section, "fredons," is, according to Littré, a musical term signifying a rapid succession of notes (similar to the English "trill"). It suggests running, or, more precisely, chasing. At this stage in the narrative, the spider pursues the insects that have become entangled in the web. The chase motif corresponds, in the musical parallel, to the essence of fugal counterpoint: each voice, as it enters, "chases" another one that "flies" away from it. Indeed, the etymology of *fugue* indicates this very notion: the word derives from the Latin *fuga*, meaning flight, or *fuite* in French.

The reference to the musical form of the fugue in the final part of the poem is complex. Not only does it evoke the scrambling spider, chasing after an insect trapped in the web, but it also constitutes a more general comment on the structure of the poem. The essence of the fugue is its "woven texture," called counterpoint. A fugue is the interweaving of melodic strands, just as the web is made of interwoven threads. The spider's creation is a metaphor of the poet's creation: *texte* derives from the Latin *textus*, woven thing, from *texere*, to weave.

Upon examination of this section's extensive language play, one discovers that the aural fusion produced by the reformation of certain words and phrases conforms, in musical terms, to the introduction of the fugal subject in the tonic key followed by its answer in the dominant key. For instance, the phrase "Sachez, quoi qu'il en soit" [Be aware, whatever the nature {of my secret paunch} may be] is taken up a few lines later, its phonetic qualities being somewhat modified: "sachet, coquille en soie" [sachet, silk cocoon]. Likewise, the phrase "de ma panse secrète" [of my secret paunch] receives a responding variation: "que ma panse sécrète" [that my paunch secretes]. Further mimicking of contrapuntal variation is provided by the footnotes to the words "je ne sois" and "échriveau" in the phrase "et bien que je ne sois qu'un échriveau" [although I may be only a spinibbler {deliberate conflation of words}]. These footnotes transform (or "transpose") the phrase into "et bien que jeune soie qu'un échrivain," "jeune soie" referring obliquely to one of the nine denotations of the noun *araignée* given by Littré: "Première soie que filent les vers à soie pour soutenir les cocons" [First silk that silkworms spin to support their cocoons or shells].

This aural fusion produced by phonetic variation is in agreement with the mixing of *jes* in the poem: the "je"-poet and the "je"-spider: the words "échriveau" and "échrivain," for example, remind the reader of the words "écheveau" (a skein, or metonymical web) and "écrivain" (maker of the *textus*, or woven thing). Puns such as "panse/pense" and "je ne sois/jeune soie" operate in a similar way, as they point to the connection between the creation of the text and the secretion of the web, and the conflation of creator and creation. As Ponge puts it at the beginning of the poem: "Sans doute le sais-je bien . . . (pour l'avoir quelque jour dévidé de moi-même? . . .) que l'araignée sécrète son fil, bave le fil de sa toile. . . ." [No doubt I know very well . . . (for having at some time unwound it from myself? . . .) that the spider secretes its thread, slobbers the thread of its web. . . .]. The poem is replete with such puns, and yet the wordplay is far from gratuitous, for the complex semantic layering it produces consistently heightens the deeper meaning of the text to such an extent, in fact, that the reader becomes increasingly convinced that this layering is the poem's ultimate subject.

In addition to the interrelationship between the various rhythms of the suite and the poem's narrative of the spider's activities, this text accomplishes the translation of Rameau's harmony into Pongian language by means of an invisible source, or "fundamental bass" that generates the various textual overtones—the etymology of the title noun itself, as discovered in the Littré dictionary. The many acoustic variations and formal analogies are, I suggest, motivated by the original distinction between these two arrangements of alphabetical "elements": *aragne* and *araignée*, that is, the

Old French words that signified respectively the spider and the thing made by the spider, its web. Modern French, on the other hand, "fuses" the two words: as always, Ponge takes into account the "épaisseur sémantique" (semantic density) of language, and the ideas of spider and web are mixed, or "sounded simultaneously" in *araignée*, since nowadays the animal is referred to by the word that originally meant its product. Littré explains the word's history as follows: "La vieille langue distinguait donc l'*aragne* et l'*araignée*; la nouvelle langue s'est appauvrie et défigurée en confondant l'ouvrière et l'oeuvre; cette confusion paraît être venue dans le XVIe s" [The old language distinguished therefore between *aragne* and *araignée*; the new language has become impoverished and disfigured by mixing up the worker and the work; this confusion seems to have occurred in the sixteenth century]. In another poem of the same collection ("La Nouvelle Araignée" [The new spider], in *GRP*, 197–200), Ponge points this out, while differing remarkably from Littré in his emotional response to it: "Dès le lever du jour il est sensible en France—bien que cela se trame dans les coins—et merveilleusement confus dans le langage, que l'araignée avec sa toile ne fasse qu'un" [As of daybreak it is noticeable in France—although it is being spun in the corners—and wonderfully confused in the language, that the spider with its web make only one]. Referring to the Renaissance by the metaphorical "lever du jour" [daybreak], the passage underscores the historical moment at which, according to Littré, the fusion took place in the language. And in order to further poeticize this "marvelous confusion" by means of formal imitation, the plural subject, "l'araignée avec sa toile" [the spider with its web], receives not the expected plural form of the verb, *fassent*, but its singular form, *fasse*.

This metonymy lies deep within the nooks and crannies of the French language: as Ponge puts it, "cela se trame dans les coins" [it spins {with the overtone of "it is being plotted"} in the corners]. Although never explicit in the poem, it is nevertheless developed throughout the text and constitutes the driving force behind its main theme: the conflation of poet (author/ spider) and poem (text/web), which is expressed by the metaphor of the spider and its activity. Viewed in this light, the self-reflexive text also effectively evokes the notion of the poet as maker, the poem as created thing, and eventually leads us back through the history of the language to the ancestral Greek source, *poiein*, to make, and therefore to a deep and fundamental comprehension of poetry as such.

Ponge appropriates Rameau's reflections, bringing them into the domain of literature, where the musician's priorities become those of the poet. The distinction drawn between the functions of melody and harmony, the latter being valorized, finds its analogue in Ponge's work in the greater importance he assigns to the paradigmatic, as opposed to the syntagmatic, dimension of language, that is, to the accumulation of associative density vertically intersecting any given point along the horizontal spoken sequence.[9] Any narrative line, unfolding in time in Ponge's work, is consistently subordinated to the intense activity taking place at the level of simultaneous semantic interrelations. This technique of poetic composition extends the text back through time, since the valorization of the paradigmatic axis necessarily draws us into the past or historical existence of words at each sequential moment of the text. This kind of textual harmony, then, echoes the ancient Greek meaning of the word *music* that Ponge so frequently invokes: "La Musique (au sens grec), c'est-à-dire . . . l'harmonie et le fonctionnement intemporels" [Music (according to the Greek meaning), that is . . . timeless harmony and functioning] ("Le Mariage en 57," in *GRL*, 141).[10] It is in this sense that no matter how forward-looking Ponge may be, no matter how modern, he can be called a classicist, for he insists on anchoring his own work in what he and others consider to be chefs d'oeuvre, or timeless works. He says as much himself in this passage where he considers the relationship between himself and Rameau: "Dans la mesure où nous avons besoin d'une étoile, nous pouvons choisir [l'oeuvre de Rameau]. . . . Elle brille toujours au Zénith! Incorporée à l'harmonie des sphères, à la musique de Pythagore" [To the extent that we need a star, we can choose {the work of Rameau}. . . . It shines always at the zenith! Incorporated into the harmony of the spheres, into the music of Pythagoras] ("La Société du génie," in *GRM*, 208). For Ponge, his own literature must be linked firmly to the Greek notion of music, and his efforts in this direction may be observed throughout his work, even in its details, for example in the title of one of his volumes: *L-y-r-e-s*. Since the title noun is in the plural, each piece of the collection is designated as an ancient and, for Ponge, highly symbolic musical instrument. And since on the auditory level there is an obviously intentional confusion (in the noble sense of the word) with the verb *lire* (to read), this title reveals once again Ponge's desire to conflate music and literature. He does so in order to build a timeless monument to cosmic harmony, as in this passage from his *Pour un Malherbe*, where the conflation is extended even more universally in praise of Malherbe's musical qualities. Malherbe's intense exploration of the material aspect of his language makes his work as indestructible as the Parthenon or the Maison Carrée in Nîmes; it links music and architecture within Ponge's particular notion of classicism:

> Que le classicisme soit la corde la plus tendue du baroque. . . . Mais encore faut-il que le baroque soit fondu dans la pierre. . . . N'importe quel

monument comportant un péristyle à colonnes évoque le plus adéquatement, dans l'ordre de l'architecture, un instrument à cordes. Car il y a, sur le devant, les colonnes tendues comme les cordes de la lyre . . . , et derrière, le temple . . . , c'est-à-dire la caisse de résonance. (*PM*, 188–89)

[Classicism is the tightest string of the baroque. . . . But the baroque must still be cast in stone. . . . Any monument consisting of a peristyle with columns evokes most appropriately, in the realm of architecture, a stringed instrument. For there is, on the front, tight columns like the strings of the lyre . . . , and behind, the temple . . . , that is, the resonance chamber.]

Echoing the root meaning of the word *harmony* itself, the "articulation" of artistic language toward the external world of nature is another preoccupation that Ponge shares with Rameau. The term by which Ponge usually designates it is *adéquation* [appropriateness {but with the etymological meaning of *adequate*, to make equal}].[11] This notion, which is also developed in the passage, involves the material aspect of artistic language—the so-called world of preexistent physical elements from which the artist chooses, and which are arranged by the artist in the formulation of the artwork. As Ponge says, the music of Rameau is three-dimensional. The language of the poet, as it is modeled on that of the musician, is a self-contained world that is homologous to the external world: the elements of the text not only signify but also function in relation to themselves, on the level of position, value, or structure, as analogues of the elements of natural phenomena. When read in a certain way, the phonetic playfulness of the passage quoted above is a good example: the word *ba-roque* provides connections with the notions of "base" or "foundation"—*ba* sounds like *bas*, "bottom," while *roque* sounds like *roc*, "rock" or "stone" *(pierre)*.

This same analogy between the internal functioning of the artwork's elements and the functioning of the elements of the phenomenal world is, according to Ponge, the driving force behind Rameau's genius: "Les ouvrages de l'esprit, tout comme ceux de la nature, croissent à la façon des cristaux. . . . Voilà ce que Rameau a compris. . . . Il veut 'étudier la nature' pour 'y faire un choix de couleurs et de nuances . . .' surprenantes avec rigueur" [The works of the mind, just like those of nature, develop as do crystals. . . . That is what Rameau understood. . . . He wants "to study nature" in order rigorously "to choose from it certain surprising colors and nuances"] ("La Société du génie," in *GRM*, 210). Remarkably, two texts and only eight pages earlier in the same volume, and in a piece entitled "Des Cristaux naturels," Ponge defines the growth of crystals to which he was referring in the passage concerning Rameau just quoted: "Il s'agit ici d'espèces homogènes, aux éléments parfaitement définis, qui croissent par juxtaposition des mêmes atomes unis entre eux par les mêmes rapports, pour apparaître enfin selon leurs contours géométriques propres" [Here it is a matter of homogeneous species, composed of perfectly defined elements, which develop by juxtaposition of the same atoms linked to each other by the same relationships, in order finally to appear with their own geometrical contours] (*GRM*, 202). These comments reveal that Ponge's particular notion of music and the artistic principles that he discerns in it correspond ultimately to the most fundamental and timeless workings of nature. There are a limited number of fundamental physical elements in the world, and their various permutations create all things. In the same way, as Rameau puts it in his *Traité de l'harmonie*:

> La division harmonique, qui selon notre système, n'est autre que la division arithmétique ne nous donne pour tout milieu harmonique que [les intervalles de] la quinte et les deux tierces; ... toute la différence que l'on y aperçoit ne provenant que de la différente disposition des sons qui composent cette quinte et ces tierces; de sorte que ce mélange arbitraire des sons auquel l'harmonie nous invite pour nous faire sentir avec plus de force la perfection de son tout par cette diversité, ne doit pas pour cela, nous faire perdre de vue un principe qui y subsiste toujours. (Rameau 1965, 29)

> [Harmonic division, which, according to our system, is nothing other than arithmetic division, provides us with only the intervals of the fifth and the two thirds for each harmonic environment; ... the whole difference that one perceives in it deriving only from the different arrangement of the tones that compose this fifth and these thirds; so that this arbitrary mixture of the sounds that the harmony proposes to us, in order to make us feel more forcefully the perfection of its entirety by means of this diversity, must not, for all that, cause us to forget a principle that is always there.]

In the final analysis, therefore, the problem of articulating a finite artistic language toward the infinite external universe, as it relates to Ponge's principle of "adéquation textuelle" [textual appropriateness] in music and in literature and in the other arts, was probably advanced most succinctly and poetically by another of Ponge's acknowledged masters, Lucretius, the Epicurean philosopher, during the first century before Christ. As mentioned in the introduction, according to Lucretius the letters of the alphabet are analogous to the atoms. Just as the different arrangements of atoms produce all the things of the external world, so the various juxtapositions of letters create the things of the linguistic world:

> All through these very lines of mine you see many elements [*elementa* {in Latin meaning simultaneously both letters and atoms}] common to many words, although you must confess that lines and words differ from one another both in meaning and in the sound of their soundings. So much can elements do, when nothing is changed but order; but elements that are the beginnings of things [that is, atoms] can bring with them more kinds of variety, from which all the various things can be produced. (*De rerum natura* 1.823–29)[12]

Ponge's reflections on Rameau lead us therefore to an understanding of the link that Ponge wishes to establish between the probably utopian tenets of his poetics and those of Rameau, and, ultimately, the cosmogonic tenets of ancient atomism. When speaking about Rameau, Ponge evokes his own metapoetic principles of "épaisseur sémantique" [semantic depth] and "adéquation textuelle" [textual appropriateness] while suggesting that his views concerning language and its role in literature are analogous to Rameau's notions about harmony and its function in music.[13] Ponge is aligning himself, as the poet who wishes to found a new rhetoric for the poetry of the future, with the musician who did in fact found a new musical rhetoric; the importance that Rameau gave to harmony was without precedent in the history of music, and he therefore set the stage for the intense exploration of harmony that was to follow. Whether the same will be true of Ponge's place in literary history remains, of course, to be seen, and the way in which he remotivates his atomistic precursors still needs to be elucidated.

L'ARAIGNÉE

EXORDE EN COURANTE.
PROPOSITION (THÈME DE LA SARABANDE).
COURANTE EN SENS INVERSE (CONFIRMATION).
SARABANDE, LA TOILE OURDIE
(GIGUE D'INSECTES VOLANT AUTOUR).
FUGUE EN CONCLUSION

Sans doute le sais-je bien... (pour l'avoir quelque jour dévidé de moi-même? ou me l'a-t-on jadis avec les linéaments de toute science appris?) que l'araignée sécrète son fil, bave le fil de sa toile... et n'a les pattes si distantes, si distinctes — la démarche si délicate — qu'afin de pouvoir ensuite arpenter cette toile — parcourir en tous sens son ouvrage de bave sans le rompre ni s'y emmêler — tandis que toutes autres bestioles non prévenues s'y emprisonnent de plus belle par chacun de leurs gestes ou cabrioles éperdues de fuite...
Mais d'abord, comment agit-elle?
Est-ce d'un bond hardi? ou se laissant tomber sans lâcher le fil de son discours, pour revenir plusieurs fois par divers chemins ensuite à son point de départ, sans

avoir tracé, tendu une ligne que son corps n'y soit passé — n'y ait tout entier participé — à la fois filature et tissage?

D'où la définition par elle-même de sa toile aussitôt conçue :

DE RIEN D'AUTRE QUE DE SALIVE PROPOS EN L'AIR MAIS AUTHENTIQUEMENT[1] TISSUS — OÙ J'HABITE AVEC PATIENCE — SANS PRÉTEXTE QUE MON APPÉTIT DE LECTEURS.

A son propos ainsi — à son image —, me faut-il lancer des phrases à la fois assez hardies et sortant uniquement de moi, mais assez solides — et faire ma démarche assez légère, pour que mon corps sans les rompre sur elles prenne appui pour en imaginer — en lancer d'autres en sens divers — et même en sens contraire par quoi soit si parfaitement tramé mon ouvrage, que ma panse[2] dès lors puisse s'y reposer, s'y tapir, et que je puisse y convoquer mes proies — vous, lecteurs, vous, attention de mes lecteurs — afin de vous dévorer ensuite en silence (ce qu'on appelle la gloire)...

Oui, soudain, d'un angle de la pièce me voici à grands pas me précipitant sur vous, attention de mes lecteurs prise au piège de mon ouvrage de bave, et ce n'est pas le moment le moins réjouissant du jeu : c'est ici que je vous pique et vous endors!

1. Var. : Mésentériquement.
2. Var. : Pensée.

SCARAMOUCHES AU CIEL[1] QUI MENEZ DEVERS MOI LE BRANLE IMPÉNITENT DE VOTRE VÉSANIE...

>Mouches et moucherons,
>abeilles, éphémères,
>guêpes, frelons, bourdons,
>cirons, mites, cousins,
>spectres, sylphes, démons,
>monstres, drôles et diables,
>gnomes, ogres, larrons,
>lurons, ombres et mânes,
>bandes, cliques, nuées,
>hordes, ruches, espèces,
>essaims, noces, cohues,
>cohortes, peuples, gens,
>collèges et sorbonnes,
>docteurs et baladins,
>doctes et bavardins,
>badins, taquins, mutins
>et lutins et mesquins,
>turlupins, célestins,
>séraphins, spadassins,
>reîtres, sbires, archers,
>sergents, tyrans et gardes,
>pointes, piques, framées,
>lances, lames et sabres,
>trompettes et clairons,
>buccins, fifres et flûtes,
>harpes, bassons, bourdons,
>orgues, lyres et vielles,
>bardes, chantres, ténors,
>strettes, sistres, tintouins,
>hymnes, chansons, refrains,
>rengaines, rêveries,
>balivernes, fredons,

1. Var. : Squadra de mouch's au ciel.

3 / Ponge and Rameau

> billevesées, vétilles,
> détails, bribes, pollens,
> germes, graines et spermes,
> miasmes, miettes, fétus,
> bulles, cendres, poussières,
> choses, causes, raisons,
> dires, nombres et signes,
> lemmes, nomes, idées,
> centons, dictons et dogmes,
> proverbes, phrases, mots,
> thèmes, thèses et gloses,

FREDONS, BILLEVESÉES, SCHÈMES EN ZIZANIE! SACHEZ, QUOI QU'IL EN SOIT DE MA PANSE SECRÈTE ET BIEN QUE JE NE SOIS[1] QU'UN ÉCHRIVEAU[2] CONFUS QU'ON EN PEUT DÉMÊLER POUR L'HEURE CE QUI SUIT : À SAVOIR QU'IL EN SORT QUE JE SUIS VOTRE PARQUE; SORT, DIS-JE, ET IL S'ENSUIT QUE BIEN QUE JE NE SOIS QUE PANSE DONC JE SUIS (SACHET, COQUILLE EN SOIE QUE MA PANSE SÉCRÈTE) VOTRE MAUVAISE ÉTOILE AU PLAFOND QUI VOUS GUETTE POUR VOUS FAIRE EN SES RAIS CONNAÎTRE VOTRE NUIT.

Beaucoup plus tard, — ma toile abandonnée — de la rosée, des poussières l'empèseront, la feront briller — la rendront de toute autre façon attirante...

Jusqu'à ce qu'elle coiffe enfin, de manière horrible ou grotesque, quelque amateur curieux des buissons ou des coins de grenier, qui pestera contre elle, mais en restera coiffé.

1. Var. : Jeune soie.
2. Var. : Échrivain.

Et ce sera la fin...
Mais fi!
De ce répugnant triomphe, payé par la destruction de mon œuvre, ne subsistera dans ma mémoire orgueil ni affliction, car (fonction de mon corps seul et de son appétit) quant à moi mon pouvoir demeure!
Et dès longtemps, — pour l'éprouver ailleurs — j'aurai fui...

THE SPIDER

> EXORDIUM IN THE FORM OF A COURANTE.
> PROPOSITION (THEME OF THE SARABAND).
> REVERSED COURANTE (CONFIRMATION).
> SARABAND, THE WEB WOVEN
> (GIGUE OF INSECTS FLYING AROUND).
> FUGUE IN CONCLUSION.

No doubt I know very well . . . (for having at some time unwound it from myself? or was I taught it once along with the lineaments of all science?) that the spider secretes its thread, slobbers the thread of its web . . . and has such distant and distinct legs—and such a delicate gait—only so that it may subsequently survey this web—run over its work of spittle in all directions without breaking it or getting entangled in it—whereas all other uninformed little creatures become all the more imprisoned in it with each of their gestures or vain maneuvers to escape . . .

But first, how does it behave?

Is it by leaping audaciously? or by allowing itself to descend without dropping the thread of its discourse, in order to come back subsequently several times by different paths to its point of departure, without having traced or stretched a single line along which its body hasn't traveled—in which it hasn't been entirely involved—at once spinning and weaving?

Whence its own definition of its newly created web:

OF NOTHING OTHER THAN SALIVA WORDS IN THE AIR BUT AUTHENTICALLY[1] WOVEN—WHERE I DWELL PATIENTLY—HAVING NO PRETEXT OTHER THAN MY HUNGER FOR READERS.

---

[1] Var.: Mesenterically.

3 / Ponge and Rameau

Thus in this connection—in its image—I must send out sentences at once sufficiently daring and coming out of myself alone, but solid enough—and have an adequately light gait, so that my body, without breaking them, may be supported by them in order to imagine others—send out more of them in different directions—and even in opposite directions thanks to which my creation may be so perfectly woven that from then on my paunch[2] may rest on them, may lurk within them, and so that I may summon my preys to them—you, readers, you, attention of my readers—in view of silently devouring you afterwards (which is known as glory) . . .

Yes, suddenly, from a corner of the room I rush forward by leaps and bounds and jump on you, attention of my readers caught in the trap of my creation of saliva, and this isn't the least thrilling moment of the game: now I bite and paralyze you!

SCARAMOUCHES IN THE SKY[3] THAT BRING BEFORE ME THE UNREPENTANT COMMOTION OF YOUR FOLLY . . .

>Flies and midges,
>bees, ephemerae,
>wasps, hornets, bumblebees,
>mites, moths, mosquitoes,
>ghosts, sylphs, demons,
>monsters, weirdos and devils,
>gnomes, ogres, thieves,
>gallants, shades and shadows,
>bands, cliques, clouds,
>hordes, hives, kinds,
>swarms, nuptials, throngs,
>cohorts, peoples, folk,
>colleges and sorbonnes,
>doctors and actors,
>eggheads and windbags,
>pranksters, teasers, mutineers
>and goblins and misers,
>pests, monks,
>seraphim, killers,
>roughnecks, punks, bowmen,

---

[2] Var.: Thought.
[3] Var.: Squadrons of flies *(mouch's)* in the sky.

3 / Ponge and Rameau

sergeants, tyrants and guards,
spikes, pikes, javelins,
lances, blades and sabers,
trumpets and bugles,
horns, fifes and flutes,
harps, bassoons, drones,
organs, lyres and hurdy-gurdies,
bards, cantors, tenors,
stretti, sistra, buzzings,
hymns, songs, refrains,
clichés, musings,
twaddle, trills,
poppycock, trivia,
details, scraps, pollen,
germs, seeds and sperm,
miasmas, crumbs, straw,
bubbles, ashes, dust,
things, causes, reasons,
statements, numbers and signs,
lemmata, counties, ideas,
centos, maxims and dogmata,
proverbs, phrases, words,
themes, theses and glosses.

TRILLS, POPPYCOCK, CRAZY SCHEMES! BE AWARE, WHATEVER THE NATURE OF MY SECRET PAUNCH MAY BE THAT WELL I AM NOTHING[4] BUT A CONFUSED SPINNIBLER[5] AND AT PRESENT ONE MAY TEASE OUT THE FOLLOWING: NAMELY THE RESULTANT FACT IS THAT I AM YOUR FATE; FATE, I SAY, AND IT FOLLOWS THAT ALTHOUGH I AM BUT PAUNCH THEREFORE I AM (SACHET, SILK COCOON THAT MY PAUNCH SECRETES) YOUR UNLUCKY STAR ON THE CEILING LYING IN WAIT FOR YOU IN ORDER TO IN ITS RAYS INTRODUCE YOU TO YOUR NIGHT.

Much later—my web forsaken—dew and dust will stiffen it, cause it to shine—make it attractive in a completely different way . . .

Until it finally winds up on somebody's head, in a horrible or grotesque fashion, some curious soul fond of bushes or the nooks and crannies of attics, who will curse it, but will remain stuck with it.

---

[4] Var.: In the original poem, the French *je ne sois* receives the variation *jeune soie* (young silk).
[5] Var.: Shcribbler.

And it will be over . . .
Bah!
Of this repugnant victory, bought with the destruction of my creation, neither arrogance nor affliction will survive in my memory, for (function of my body alone and its appetite) as far as I myself am concerned my power endures!
And—so as to test it elsewhere—I will have long since fled . . .

4
Ponge and Atomism

We have seen that Ponge's poetic views and methods come into focus through a series of productive intellectual and artistic encounters. His poetic materialism stands partly in opposition to idealism, transcendental metaphysics, and the aligned notion of music as a disembodied art. On the one hand, the dialogue that his work cultivates with Plato and the Bible and his reformulation of Rameau's musical theories constitute a strategic subversion and/or conversion of these philosophies and art for use within the context of his own poetic values. On the other hand, he expresses these same principles by references to ancient and modern atomistic theories, which he supports elsewhere but which he must nevertheless distill into reusable material for his textual constructions.

In his "Texte sur l'électricité" (Texte on electricity), for example, Ponge expresses the opinion that even the most recent scientific developments are rooted in the ancients' understanding of natural phenomena. While showing that he is familiar with the work of prominent contemporary physicists and mathematicians such as Bohr, Broglie, Einstein, Heisenberg, Planck, and Poincaré, he maintains that it is not the originality of the modern point of view that impresses him most, but the similarities between ancient theories and the current positions that subsume them:

> Certes, j'ai retenu aussi et la loi de Planck, ... et le principe d'incertitude, et la relativité de l'Espace et du Temps, et la notion de l'Espace courbe, voire l'hypothèse de l'extension indéfinie de l'univers.
> Mais, en fin de compte, ... c'est la ressemblance de cette figure du monde avec celle que nous ont présentée Thalès ou Démocrite qui me frappe, plutôt que sa nouveauté.
> Lorsque je regarde, par exemple, un schéma de la course des électrons libres, de leurs imprévisibles zigzags et de leur lent entraînement concomitant dans ce que nous appelons un courant électrique, je ne vois là rien qui ne me rappelle, compte tenu de la notion de quantum d'action et

du principe d'incertitude — qui ne font que le confirmer —, le fameux *clinamen* de Démocrite et d'Epicure, appliqué aux corpuscules qu'ils avaient fort bien conçus. (*GRL*, 160–61)

[Of course I also remember Planck's law, . . . the uncertainty principle, and the relativity of Space and Time, as well as the idea of the curvature of Space, and even the hypothesis of the indefinite extension of the universe.

But after all is said and done, . . . rather than its originality, it is the similarity between this picture of the world and the one that Thales and Democritus proposed to us that strikes me.

For example, when I look at a diagram of the trajectories of free electrons, of their unforeseeable zigzags, and of their being slowly and concurrently pulled into what we call an electric current, I see nothing in it that does not bring to mind, even taking into account the quantum idea of action and the uncertainty principle—which only confirm it—the famous *clinamen* of Democritus and Epicurus, applied to the particles that they had so clearly imagined.]

These laudatory remarks about the ancient Greek atomists Democritus and Epicurus are soon complemented by the following superlative praise of their heir, the Latin poet Lucretius:

Et puis, je relis Lucrèce et je me dis qu'on n'a jamais rien écrit de plus beau; que rien de ce qu'il a avancé, dans aucun ordre, ne me paraît avoir été sérieusement démenti, mais au contraire plutôt confirmé. (*GRL*, 161)

[And then I reread Lucretius, and I tell myself that nobody has ever written anything more beautiful; that nothing of what he put forward, in any category, seems to me to have been seriously refuted, but on the contrary rather confirmed.]

For a contemporary poet like Ponge, who is so intensely interested in intellectual history, and whose initial postulate, as Sartre maintained (1947, 248), corresponds to that of science, it is of great significance that ancient Greek atomism is the only prescientific system that twentieth-century science can and does uphold as true to fact.[1] Equally consequential is the point that, although Epicurean physics coincides almost perfectly with our modern understanding of the atomic structure of matter, it was devised without the technological instruments that we possess today, and that allow us to actually observe phenomena described by Epicurus, who was aided only by his reason, intuition, and imagination.

The importance that Epicurus gave to intuition and imagination in his discussions of the numerous possible explanations of phenomena is an aspect of his philosophy that may strike one as essentially poetic.[2] It is this kind of scientific understanding of the nature of things as inseparable not only from reason but also from creative participation that appeals to Ponge, and that he would claim for his own undertaking, thereby reconciling poetry and science. Commenting on this relationship during an interview with Philippe Sollers, Ponge remarks:

> [S]i la science fait appel à quelque chose comme l'hypothèse, ... à quelque chose qui dépend de l'esprit humain dans son fonctionnement le plus secret, le plus profond, c'est-à-dire du rêve, ... de la fantaisie, du sommeil (quand Newton a-t-il trouvé? quand il s'est allongé sous un pommier ...), ... si la science admet que l'hypothèse est importante, alors, pourquoi pas tout le reste: disons, d'un mot les "intuitions"? (*EPS*, 130–31)

> [If science makes use of something like hypothesis, ... of something that depends on the most secret, the deepest mechanisms of the human mind, namely dream, fantasy, and sleep (when did Newton make his discovery? when he was lying under an apple tree ...), ... if science admits that hypothesis is important, then why not all the rest: let's say, in a word, "intuitions"?]

The accomplishment of Epicurus, and its revivification in the work of Lucretius, exemplifies just this kind of poetic/scientific compatibility, and legitimates Ponge's effort to create a poetic cosmogony built on a reunion of reason and intuition within the human spirit. Ponge's work would abate this counterproductive antinomy embedded in Western civilization (see *EPS*, 131); and his texts would thereby help himself and his readers to overcome the widespread modern sense of a tragic division between nature and the individual.[3]

The connection between poetry and science, so admirable in the work of Lucretius, is, according to Ponge, anchored in our very patterns of thought. We tend to see the world through the rhetorical devices we use, figures of speech that derive from Euclidean geometry and the worldview that it reflects. The rhetorical ellipsis is linked to the geometrical ellipse, hyperbole to the hyperbola, parable to the parabola (*GRL*, 163).[4] But modern science has moved beyond Euclid's formulations, and poetry must keep abreast of this change in our understanding of reality by developing new, parallel forms of thought and expression. Ponge's understanding of modern atomistic science is indissociable from his knowledge of ancient atomism, and it is in connection with the maturation of this worldview and its expression that he conceptualizes his own poetic language. It is not a matter of forgetting, but of remotivating the old structures. In this way, Ponge's poetics would be the springboard for a future poetry, one better able to render the workings of nature within the perpetually evolving context of human formulations concerning the external world:

> C'est quand nous nous enfonçons, nous aussi, dans notre matière: les sons significatifs. Sans souci des formes anciennes et les refondant dans la masse, comme on fait des vieilles statues, pour en faire des canons, des balles... puis, quand il le faut, à nouveau des Colonnes, selon les exigences du Temps.
> Ainsi formerons-nous un jour peut-être les nouvelles Figures, qui nous permettront de nous confier à la Parole pour parcourir l'Espace courbe, l'Espace non-euclidien. (*GRL*, 163)

> [It occurs when we too plunge into our material: meaningful sounds. Without worrying about ancient forms, and melting them down into a block, as is done with old statues in order to make canons and bullets from them ... then, when necessary, new Columns, according to the demands of Time.
> In this way, perhaps one day we will create the new Figures that will allow us to have faith in the Word in order to travel through curved Space, non-Euclidean Space.]

In Ponge's analogical scheme, the poet, like other technicians, creates by means that are comparable to the dialectical mechanisms of nature itself: death and destruction lead to life and construction. Nothing is lost in this vast recycling process; one thing's elemental remains are extracted and then rearranged in the formation of another thing.

Ponge's reworking of his precursors' writings involves significant aspects of Lucretius's explanations of the mechanisms of nature, one of which is the doctrine of the *clinamen*. According to this principle, atoms may unpredictably and spontaneously swerve out of the straight lines in which they travel downward through the void, then come into contact with other elements, thereby making things out of their associations. This crucial addendum to the materialistic determinism of Democritus is the part of Epicurean physics on which free will is founded: the atoms are propelled by nothing other than their own interior force (see Marx 1967, 80ff., and Nizan 1938, 96). Harold Bloom has associated the term *clinamen* with his notion of "misprision," and has applied it to what he considers to be the psychologically motivated deviation of authors with respect to their literary forebears (see Bloom 1973, 5, 14, 30, 85, 88). This helps explain a certain, characteristically Western, perspective on artistic "originality." Bloom's use of the word does not, however, completely describe the role played by the *clinamen* in Ponge's work, because the poet's worldview is fundamentally atomistic; both his notion of poetry as such and his poetic practice derive from this philosophical attitude.

This brings us to yet another major point of contact between Ponge and Lucretius, which must be considered in conjunction with the *clinamen*: the tenets of the Epicurean cosmogony, according to which nothing is created out of nothing, and nothing returns to nothing. When Ponge departs from his precursors, this deviation is itself an analogue, in the homologous world of texts, of the atomic mechanism of the *clinamen*. That is, Ponge does not hide; rather he displays his variation in order to depict the origin of his writings in previous writings. His *Pour un Malherbe* makes this abundantly clear. The poet's use of his precursors in the development of his own work is a textual rendition of the evolution of phenomena in the external world, where one thing arises through the processes of extraction and rearrangement of another's elemental remains. The particular way in which he assimilates his precursors presents certain idiosyncrasies, but in fact it runs parallel to nature's conservation of species, for it is always a remotivation in view of extending the traditions of Epicurean philosophy and literary materialism that Ponge locates in the poetry of his acknowledged masters. Lucretius does not claim philosophical originality, but does assert that his poetic rewriting of Epicureanism is that of a pioneer.[5] Just so, it is Ponge's regeneration of these views, and not the views themselves, that is innovative.

Ponge's notion of "originality" diverges from the present-day norm, for the analogical connection he maintains between the subject of the text and the text itself requires that he be original only in his very "unoriginality." If his texts are to present a homologue of the external world, they can succeed only if they exhibit their derivation; for, according to the Epicurean vision, there is no such thing as creation ex nihilo. In other words, absolute originality is impossible; and the atom, according to the doctrine of the *clinamen*, does not deviate in order to set itself apart from, but to unite with, other atoms within a composite body, of which it is only one of myriad subordinate elements.

Ponge's interest in atomistic theories is firmly implanted in his knowledge of the ancients, but it also encompasses more recent advances. Indeed, the unfolding of the atomistic intuition from ancient to modern times, from the concept of an ultimately solid, indivisible, and utterly discontinuous *atomos* (the Greek word used by Epicurus, meaning "uncuttable") to the idea of a subdivisible atom, is one of the poet's preoccupations. His *Le Parti pris des choses*, for instance, includes two pieces—"Pluie" (Rain) and "Le Galet" (The pebble)—which subsume ancient atomistic theories while adding modern notions to them. "Pluie" and "Le Galet" are, respectively, the first and last pieces of the collection; they can therefore be regarded as forming its evolutionary limits, which, given Ponge's interest in the development of atomism, makes an examination of the relationship between these two poems especially productive.

Ancient atomism used the metaphor of rain to illustrate the fall of atoms in parallel, straight lines. In Lucretius's poem, this image suggests the Epicurean theory of atoms falling through the void. The problem with this model is that it does not allow for the creation of phenomena; it excludes the possibility of interatomic contact and, consequently, the conjunction of primal elements within a composite body (see *De rerum natura* 2.220–24). For the atomists, matter is eternal; it and the other ultimate reality, the void, constitute the universe.

In Ponge's "Pluie," we can see the ancient metaphor: it is into a courtyard—an empty space within a building—that an observer watches the raindrops (atoms) fall: "La pluie, dans la cour où je la regarde tomber, descend à des allures très diverses" [Rain, in the courtyard where I watch it fall, descends at very different speeds] (*TP*, 35). Yet this image, consistent is some ways with the primitive Epicurean notion, is altered in Ponge's poem. Rain does not move through a vacuum in which all things, regardless of weight, would have equal velocity, as Epicurus maintained as regards the atoms.

Ponge, like Lucretius, confronts theory with practice. Rain is, as Ponge puts it, "une fraction intense du météore pur" [an intense fraction of the pure meteor], that is, the metaphor of rain brings the concept of atoms falling through the void into the earth's atmosphere. Reading etymologically, the reader's conceptual focal point passes, like a meteorite, from the vacuum of outer space through the earth's atmosphere: the original meaning of the Greek *meteoron* is "astronomical phenomena," from *meteoros*, "high in the air." But it has come to mean "atmospheric phenomena." Rain is a single species, or "fraction," of this plural generic. The linguistic matter of *météore* already includes the notion of intensity expressed by Ponge's adjective, "une fraction intense." In fact, it is a "fraction" of *meteoros* itself, which is broken down into *meta-* (intensifier) + *aeirein*, to raise. Within the earth's atmosphere, which is not a vacuum, rain falls at different speeds, since raindrops are relatively light or heavy. In the poem, although it falls at different speeds, the rain is divided into different sections (at the center of the courtyard, and near the left and right walls); the raindrops within each section all fall at the same speed. At the center, the lighter raindrops form a metaphorical "rideau (ou réseau)" [curtain (or network)], but, oddly enough, this curtain is "discontinu" [discontinuous], that is, the parts that make it are perceived as separate. Likewise, the heavier raindrops nearer the walls are "individuées" [individualized]. As long as they are moving vertically, the raindrops are individualized and compared to separate things of varying size and weight: "un grain de blé" [a grain of wheat], "un pois" [a pea], "une bille" [a marble].

This view of rain corresponds to Epicurus's perspective: the metaphor of falling raindrops illustrates the theory of atoms falling through the void where they can never catch up with each other and create things. This is why the slight deviation, or *clinamen*, of the atoms is required—without it, nature would never have produced anything at all. And indeed, in Ponge's "Pluie" it is only when the rain moves across the slightly sloping roof and through the adjoining gutter that its individual particles make bodies of water: the discontinuous drops of rain combine to form a continuous stream or, as it pours out from the gutter, a thin, roughly braided thread. At the end of the text, this physical continuum is brought into relief when, by falling to the ground, the collision resolves it into the tiny particles from which it derived; just so, in the linguistic world of the text, the image of rain as a *filet* (thin thread) motivates the diminutive of *aiguille* (needle)—the things with which the elements of the metaphorical "curtain (or network)" were woven together:

> Sur des tringles, sur les accoudoirs de la fenêtre la pluie court horizontalement tandis que sur la face inférieure des mêmes obstacles elle se suspend en berlingots convexes.... De la goutière attenante où elle coule avec la contention d'un ruisseau creux sans grande pente, elle choit tout à coup en un filet parfaitement vertical, assez grossièrement tressé, jusqu'au sol où elle se brise et rejaillit en aiguillettes brillantes. (*TP*, 35–36)

> [Along taeniae, along the windowsills the rain runs horizontally, whereas from the underside of the same obstacles it hangs like convex candies.... From the adjoining gutter through which it flows in a shallow, concentrated stream hardly sloping, it suddenly plunges like a thin, perfectly vertical thread, rather roughly braided, until it hits the ground and shatters, splashing up like shining little needles.]

This presentation takes the metaphor of rain out of the deterministic mode characteristic of Democritus; and the image is remotivated in an Epicurean context: the doctrine of the *clinamen*, or swerving of the atoms, is implicit in the oblique, confluent behavior of rain, the individual particles of which ("berlingots") coexist with compound bodies of water ("ruisseau," "filet").

If compared to the final piece of the collection ("Le Galet"), "Pluie" appears as an oracular statement concerning the evolution of the concept of the atom as it is understood by twentieth-century science, that is, as the synthesis of corpuscular and wavelike aspects of matter, of the discontinuous and the continuous. "Le Galet" maps the breaking up into increasingly smaller and smaller particles of an "enormous ancestor"—a great rock:

> Tous les rocs sont issus par scissiparité d'un même aïlleul énorme. De ce corps fabuleux l'on ne peut dire qu'une chose, savoir que hors des limbes il n'a point tenu debout. (*TP*, 104)

> [All rocks stem by fission from a single enormous ancestor. Concerning this legendary body, one can say only this: outside of limbo it did not remain intact.]

This progressive parceling process is intimately associated with the liquid element. From the imposing, massive solidity of an ancestral boulder, innumerable less massive entities are splintered. We proceed chronologically through the text from singular boulder to plural, smaller rocks, pebbles, and, beyond, to grains of sand on the beach—all of which are "genealogically" connected to the boulder-father. The prototype boulder, looming above and separate from the waves, is transformed, over time, into a multitude of small particles, still solid or corpuscular yet inextricably associated with, even enveloped by, the sea—a paragon of fluidity, by whose erosive action this epitome of solidity is worn down:

> Enfin, de jour en jour plus petit mais toujours sûr de sa forme, aveugle, solide et sec dans sa profondeur, son caractère est donc de ne pas se laisser confondre mais plutôt réduire par les eaux. Aussi, lorsque vaincu il est enfin du sable, l'eau n'y pénètre pas exactement comme à la poussière. Gardant alors toutes les traces, sauf justement celles du liquide, qui se borne à pouvoir effacer sur lui celles qu'y font les autres, il laisse à travers lui passer toute la mer, qui se perd en sa profondeur sans pouvoir en aucune façon faire avec lui de la boue. (*TP*, 114)

> [Finally, day after day smaller but still sure of its shape, blind, solid and dry in its depths, its nature therefore is such that it avoids becoming fused with the waters but rather is reduced by them. Consequently, when in the end, defeated, it is sand, water doesn't penetrate it exactly as it does dust. Then keeping all the traces, except precisely those of liquid, which is limited to washing away the marks that the others make, it allows itself to be traversed by the entire sea, which gets lost in its depths without in any way being able to transform it into mud.]

Le Parti pris des choses, therefore, depicts in its framing the dissolution of the ancient atomistic *atomos* into ever smaller subatomic particles. It points to the duality at the heart of matter, and to the reconciliation accomplished by modern wave mechanics, which explains certain phenomena that are incompatible with classical physics (see Broglie 1937, 44, 77–78, 242). And the analogical unfolding of the collection with respect to the evolution of atomism is reinforced by the midpoint poem, "Bords de mer" (Seashores), which concerns the meeting of solid and liquid.

It is significant that, in the final poem, "Le Galet," Ponge expresses his preference for the relative solidity and considerable dimensions of the pebble over the grains of sand, thereby pointing to what we may call his conservatism:

> Le vent le plus fort pour déraciner un arbre ou démolir un édifice, ne peut déplacer un galet. Mais comme il fait voler la poussière alentour, c'est ainsi que parfois les furets de l'ouragan déterrent quelqu'une de ces bornes du hasard à leurs places quelconques depuis des siècles sous la couche opaque et temporelle du sable. (*TP*, 113)

> [Winds strong enough to uproot a tree or demolish an edifice cannot move a pebble. But as they make dust fly all about, in this way sometimes hurricane ferrets dislodge one of these boundary stones of fate from some spot or other that they have occupied for centuries under the opaque and temporal layer of sand.]

This conservatism has a relation to the ancient atomistic view of Epicurus and Lucretius, which posits a necessary "least part," or *atomos*, upon which all phenomena must be built. Analogically, this least part in Ponge's construction of a textual phenomenon is the poetry of Lucretius, to which, through the Malherbian trunk, Ponge's work is connected, as a leaf is linked to the indispensable roots of a tree.[6]

Malherbe is described throughout Ponge's *Pour un Malherbe* as being solid and, indeed, indestructible, hence as eternal as the *atomos*. His words are said to be the rocklike, necessary foundation of all posterior French language, literature, civilization, and spirit. Around his work revolve all recent manifestations of French literature, like electrons orbiting around an atomic nucleus. Seen in this light, the following passage from *Pour un Malherbe* may be understood not only as a materialistic vision of the external world but also of the analogous literary world:

> Aujourd'hui... j'ai songé à un poème évoquant le Monde où nous sommes plongés, où nous baignons comme un petit rouage, minuscule mais indis-

pensable, ridicule mais précieux et sacré; comme un petit rouage perdu (exactement à l'endroit qui convient) dans le boîtier d'une machine grandiose et complexe, formidable et subtile . . . tant ses mécanismes sont variés et déliés. . . . Toute de la même matière (hydrates de carbone + quelques métaux, alias pierres précieuses, principes des couleurs) mais variée, modifiée à l'infinie, selon la figure et la vitesse, la longueur d'onde de chaque élément de ces corps simples à la place qu'ils occupent dans le système solaire dont ils font partie. (*PM*, 74)

[Today . . . I dreamt of a poem evoking the World in which we are immersed, in which we bathe like a little cog, miniscule but indispensable, ridiculous but precious and sacred; like a little cog lost (exactly at the appropriate spot) in the casing of a grandiose and complex machine, tremendous and subtle . . . so varied and nimble are its mechanisms. . . . All of the same matter (carbohydrates + some metals, alias gemstones, principles of the colors) but varied, infinitely modified, according to the geometrical figure and the speed, the wavelength of each element of these discrete particles in the spot that they occupy in the solar system of which they are components.]

This excerpt presents a poeticized version of a certain modern view of the atom that Ponge finds particularly fascinating; as he tells us in the "Texte sur l'électricité": "J'ai été profondément marqué par la très-frappante image, proposée par Henri Poincaré, qui, rapprochant les deux infinis, nous fait concevoir l'atome comme un système solaire et ses électrons libres comme des comètes" [I was deeply impressed by the very striking image, proposed by Henri Poincaré, that, by bringing the two infinites together, makes us imagine the atom like a solar system and its free electrons like comets] (*GRL*, 160). The above quotation from *Pour un Malherbe* includes several references to this model, which is sometimes called the "Bohr atom," after the Danish physicist who developed it around 1912. Since it explains the atom through an analogy with the solar system, this paradigm, as Ponge says, fuses two Pascalian infinites ("les deux infinis")—the exceedingly large solar system and the immeasurably small atom. A kind of microcosm, it reduces the universe to an infinitesimal speck, and, reciprocally, what is normally considered on the microscopic level is expanded to astronomic proportions. The indispensable ancient *atomos* is nevertheless preserved, yet relocated in the image of the sun-nucleus, whose gravitational pull, or counterbalancing electric charge, is necessary in order to maintain the planets, or electrons, in their orbits around it. The modern scientific model at once incorporates and supersedes its precursor, and Ponge's relation to Malherbe, which is implicit in his poetic appropriation of the solar system-atom, constitutes an artistic parallel in which Malherbe is a nucleus and Ponge himself an electron.

It is the electrons that create interatomic bonds, which lead to the construction of molecules and therefore to the world of things that they produce; and the cohesion of a coinciding, poetic world is one of the goals to be accomplished by Ponge's poetics. His endeavor to render modern atomistic notions in a common language reveals an ethical ambition that correlates with that of Epicurus and Lucretius. The ancient atomists strived to liberate humans from the fear of the gods, which resulted from mythology; and Ponge believes that a similar apprehension grips us today when we consider scientific explanations of the world, which are expressed in a specialized language that is, for most of us, entirely baffling. Instead of mysterious gods, we now confront the key terms of modern physics:

> Les grandes déesses à nouveau sont assises, suscitées par l'homme sans doute, mais il ne les conçoit qu'avec terreur. Elles s'appellent Angström, Année-Lumière, Noyau, Fréquence, Onde, Énergie, Fonction-Psi, Incertitude. (*GRL*, 162)[7]

> [The great goddesses are once again installed, created no doubt by humans, who, however, imagine them only with terror. They are called Angstrom, Light-Year, Nucleus, Frequency, Wave, Energy, Psi Function, Uncertainty.]

Ponge nevertheless insists that, unlike the language of other technicians, the language of poets must be considered apart. In the confusing jumble—Ponge calls it "La Tour de Babel" [The Tower of Babel]—of so many recondite signifying systems, only our shared speech stands a chance of being understood by everyone, and therefore of bringing us all together—with one notable caveat:

> Ses matériaux, en effet, empruntés au bien commun de tous: la Parole, sont pour le moins autant que sensibles *intelligibles*: à condition d'être bien agencés. (*GRL*, 151)

> [Its materials, moreover, borrowed from the common possession of us all—Speech—are at least as *intelligible* as they are perceptible, provided they are well arranged.]

Ponge's insistence, in the passage just quoted, on the poet's skillful arrangement of linguistic matter recalls the many references, both implicit and explicit, that are made in his work to the primal analogy between the nature of things and the nature of words that appears several times in Lucretius's didactic poem. This analogy is of great relevance for Ponge's notion of a poetic materialism because it shows that the text, like a thing in the external world, is the result of a particular distribution of physical elements. When the arrangement of these shared elements is even the slightest bit different (as in the words *fires* and *firs* in the following passage), the characteristics of the phenomenon—thing or word—change also. Lucretius expresses the concept as follows (the Latin *elementa* [elements] can mean both atoms and letters):

> It is often of very great importance with what and in what position these same first-beginnings are held in union, and what motions they impart and receive mutually, and how the same elements a little changed in their relations create fires and firs. Just as the words themselves too consist of elements a little changed, when we mark fires and firs with a distinct name. (*De rerum natura* 1.908–14)

According to this passage, the author makes texts just as nature produces things, that is, by the permutation of preexistent elements. The author's inventive act, as well as the product of this act, is analogous to natural processes and phenomena. This ancient materialistic view of the poet and the poem informs Ponge's work. It is used repeatedly, especially whenever it is a question of defining his own distinctive artistic and ethical perspective.

Whereas in Lucretius's poem the permutation of atomic elements is analogous to the arrangement of letters within words, in Ponge's work the elemental unit is sometimes expanded to the level of the text. For instance, his piece titled "Strophe" (Stanza and strophe) deals not only with natural elements, but also with an essential formal element of poetic construction, the strophe. While closely aligning his text, both thematically and technically, with Lucretius's analogy, Ponge exploits the etymology of the word *strophe*. Motivated by the title word's derivation from the Greek *strophe*, a turning, "Strophe" is a text on the act of turning, which becomes a metaphor of the cyclical processes of nature as they are reflected in the analogically formal and semantic world of the poem. Recalling Lucretius's analogy, the homologous permutation of letters can be seen in "Strophe," where Ponge's readers find the anagrammatically decomposed elements of the word *tournure* within the place where the elemental remains, or ashes of the dead are gathered—the *urne*, which contains natural essences, is, as Ponge says, a "sobre jarre à teneur de toute la nature" [Sober jar whose contents are nature as a whole] (*Proêmes*, in *TP*, 195). Here, the urn is said to be that of *strophe* ("ton urne"), and it is replaced by the semantic equivalent of an irreducible natural element—the primary meaning of *strophe* (that is, "tournure")—as its material, alphabetical elements are subsequently recycled: "Strophe! Heureux, subrogée à *ton urne* abattue, / A de tacites bords lorsque tu prends *tournure*. . . ." [Strophe! Happy, substituted for your weakened *urn* {anagrammatic decomposition}, / With silent edges as you take *shape* {recomposition}. . . .] (ibid.; emphasis added).

Ponge's texts show the similarity between the atom and the elemental in language; and the words of his poetry, like the atoms of twentieth-century science, are sometimes subdivisible into significant parts. During his interviews with Philippe Sollers, for instance, Ponge explains that in his poem, "Le Volet, suivi de sa scholie" (The shutter, followed by its explication) (*GRP*, 117–21), even individual letters of the word *stabat* have meaning:

> Stabat. (Les deux "t", naturellement, de "stabat" sont les verticales qui indiquent le fusil tenu dans la position du "Présentez, armes!") Et les deux "a" ce sont les deux gonds, ou les deux mains qui attachent le fusil au corps du soldat, le volet au mur de la maison. (*EPS*, 144)

> [Stabat. (Naturally, the two *t*s of "stabat" are the vertical lines that indicate the rifle held in the position of the command "Present, arms!") And the two *a*s are the two hinges, or the two hands that join the rifle to the soldier's body, the shutter to the wall of the house.]

Here, Ponge expands the Lucretian point of view considerably; Lucretius never speaks of letters as signs, but only of their physical arrangement that produces the signifying word. Ponge sees more microscopically; for him, a letter is not only a material component; the letter's physical characteristics may function on the semiotic level as well.[8]

Another way in which Ponge elaborates Lucretius's paradigm may be observed in his *Le Savon* (Soap). Confronted with his friends' incomprehension of this text, the poet decided to recast it, as he explains in the following passage:

> Le silence de Paulhan, les réserves de Camus me firent beaucoup réfléchir, et j'en vins peu à peu, afin de rendre mes intentions plus claires, aussi claires que possible, sans *rien* changer pourtant au texte dont je m'étais satisfait, sans y ajouter *rien*, pas la moindre phrase, pas le moindre mot, à concevoir une sorte de distribution des éléments de ce texte, je veux dire des différentes propositions (au sens grammatical) dont il était composé.
> Une sorte de distribution, au sens où un metteur en scène (ce

personnage que vous appelez, vous, le *régisseur*) distribue à diverses voix, à divers personnages, le *texte* qu'il a mission de transformer en *spectacle*. (*S*, 38)

[Paulhan's silence, Camus's misgivings made me think very seriously, and, in order to make my intentions clearer, as clear as possible, without however changing *anything* in the text with which I was satisfied, without adding *anything* to it, not the least phrase, not the least word, little by little I resorted to imagining a kind of distribution of the elements of this text, I mean of the different propositions (in the grammatical sense) of which it was composed.

A kind of distribution, in the way that a theater director (this character that you out there call the *stage manager*) distributes to different voices, to different characters, the *text* that he is in charge of transforming into a *show*.]

As implied in the passage quoted above, Ponge's script version of *Le Savon* resulted from Camus's inability to grasp the poet's intentions.[9] Perhaps because Camus was at the time involved in theatrical productions, Ponge took the elements from the first part of the book, which had been distilled into the very brief "Prélude au savon" (36), then distributed them to the dramatis personae of a new section, "Saynète ou momon" (41–49). In this section, Ponge reuses Lucretius's analogy by expanding the "elements" from letters to phrases and sentences; moreover, in the passage quoted above, he specifies that they are not elements of a word, as in Lucretius's explanations, but of a text.

Lucretius showed that the same atoms make different compound bodies through a comparison with the distribution of the same letters shared by different words. Here, Ponge goes a step further, and demonstrates that when the same textual elements are introduced into the literary equivalent of a different body—a new genre—they take on new meaning relative to the new context. The elements of Ponge's text are therefore taken out of the prose-poem format typical of his writings, and are presented again, accompanied by indications concerning tone of voice, gestures, props, costumes, lighting, music, and sound effects; and, of course, they are spoken by different characters. A number of minor changes on the level of punctuation also occur (what was a statement becomes a question, etc.). But the text, as Ponge insists above, remains essentially the same. These slight modifications reveal certain aspects of, and interrelations between, the elements. They shed light not only on the nature of the text and textual creation as residing in the repetition of the same elements within changing contexts, but also on the essence of the text's subject: soap itself, as reflected by the text's incessant repetition of the same formal elements, always "says" the same thing wherever it may be. As Ponge explains:

> Il y a beaucoup à dire à propos du savon. Exactement tout ce qu'il raconte de lui-même, lorsqu'on l'agace avec de l'eau, d'une certaine façon....
>   Naturellement, c'est toujours la même chose qu'il dit. Et il le dit indifféremment à quiconque. Il s'exprime de la même façon avec tout le monde. (*S*, 35)

> [There is a lot to say about soap. Precisely everything that it tells about itself, when one excites it with water, in a certain way....
>   Naturally, it always says the same thing. And it says it indifferently to anyone. It expresses itself in the same way with everyone.]

It is possible to understand the theatrical version of *Le Savon* in the framework of Ponge's interest in the link between scientific and poetic developments. As those who were uninitiated into the peculiar new scientific language were sure to find the dynamics of the subatomic particles unfathomable, it was helpful to illustrate it by comparison to another, more easily visualized model, such as the solar system.[10] For a similar reason, Ponge's distribution of textual elements was presented as a theater play in order to, perhaps ironically, "popularize" his text for those who were not familiar enough with the new poetic rhetoric that he was trying to develop.

The basic Lucretian analogy between the permutation of atoms in the things of the external world and that of letters in the words of the textual world is appropriated by Ponge in the development of his new rhetoric, but its application is transposed to a different, yet parallel goal. Whereas Lucretius developed his analogies in order to illustrate the workings of nature, Ponge remotivates them; in his work, they are used to explain the nature of the poetic text. In fact, the two terms of the proportion have been inverted: what, in Lucretius's work, was the "theme" of the analogy is now, in Ponge's work, the "phore," and vice versa. Instead of saying, with Lucretius, things are like words, Ponge says words are like things. The status of atomistic theory in Ponge's conceptualization of his own writings is therefore a kind of analogical formalism.

Lucretius's analogy between things and words is profoundly appealing to Ponge, for thanks to this analogy the text does what it says; it effectively reproduces the external world in the world of language, thereby establishing the text as a homologue of the thing that is its subject. In this way, the text acquires a formal reality that is parallel to that of the phenomenal world. For example, in order to refute Anaxagoras's belief that wood contains fire, Lucretius writes: "non est lignis tamen insitus ignis" [but fire is not implanted in the wood] (*De rerum natura* 1.901). The letters of the word *ignis* (fire) are also present in the word *lignis* (wood). This physical presentation clarifies the atomistic view that it is not fire itself that is in wood, but atoms capable of making fire, just as the letters of *ignis* are in *lignis*. The specific arrangement of the text's physical elements has an expressive value that cannot be reduced to the meaning of its words alone.

Ponge reworks Lucretius's concept in the context of his own project when he talks about the text's *adéquation*; the literary work viewed as a homologue of nature, which is prevalent in Ponge's writings, derives from Lucretius' analogy, which Ponge understands as meaning that the text proceeds from its own interior laws, not from laws imposed on it from an external source:

> Il faut que les compositions que vous ne pouvez faire qu'à l'aide de ces sons significatifs, de ces mots, de ces verbes, soient arrangées de telle façon qu'elles imitent la vie des objets du monde extérieur. Imitent, c'est-à-dire qu'elles aient au moins une complexité et une présence égales. Une épaisseur égale.... On ne peut pas entièrement, on ne peut rien faire passer d'un monde à l'autre [du monde du language au monde extérieur], mais il faut, pour qu'un texte, quel qu'il soit, puisse avoir la prétention de rendre compte d'un objet du monde extérieur, il faut au moins qu'il atteigne, lui, à la réalité dans son propre monde, dans le monde des textes, qu'il ait une réalité dans le monde des textes. ("La Pratique de la littérature," in *GRM*, 276)

> [The compositions that you can create only with the help of these meaningful sounds, of these words, of these verbs, must be arranged in such a way that they imitate the life of objects in the external world. Imitate, that is to say that they should have at least an equal complexity and presence. An equal depth.... One can never {do so} completely, one cannot make anything cross from one world into the other {that is, from the world of language to the external world}, for a text, whatever it may be, to be able to aspire to giving an account of an object in the external world, it is necessary at least that it attain to reality in its own world, that it have a reality in the world of texts.]

Such views on poetry constitute a reaction against what Ponge believes to be the arbitrary and destructive distinction between body and soul, reason and intuition. This reaction corresponds to Ponge's rejection of artistic practices that are supported by the ideologies against which he rebels, for they would orient the artwork too much toward ideas, thereby minimizing its semiotic aspects and separating it from the physical world. Since Ponge believes that this divorce of the artwork and the external world brings about catastrophic ethical consequences, he endeavors to preserve an analogical connection between the Word and the World—a Wor(l)d.

Ponge's relationship to Lucretius involves not only references to his analogical explanations of natural phenomena, or the reality of the extra-linguistic world, but also to a product of language, that is, a textual reality. His references to Lucretius's *De rerum natura* are, of course, part of the general process of the transfer of knowledge from civilization to civilization, but during this process a poetic transmutation occurs. By this intertextual link, the poet intentionally anchors his work in a materialistic poetic tradition, and connects his modern perspective to ancient formulations concerning atomic nature and its relationship to the nature of the text.

5
How the Text Rewrites its Atomic Structure

Through analyzing the function of atomistic theories in Ponge's poetics, we realize that the poet's notion of textual adequacy, or appropriateness, is analogically linked to the extralinguistic processes of nature. There is also an interlinguistic proportion that occurs between Ponge (the French language), Lucretius (Latin), and Epicurus (Greek): Ponge is to Lucretius what Lucretius was to Epicurus. The rapport is maintained on the intertextual level as well: by digesting the work of Epicurus, that is, through decomposing and then rearranging its elements, Lucretius nourished his own poem, and Ponge makes his own poetry out of principles that he extracts from Lucretius's work.

Ponge's poetry displays its derivation from these precursors' writings because it would figure, in the homologous world of texts, the Epicurean view of the external world, according to which there is no creation out of nothing. As one thing stems from another, so one language grows from another—just as one text sprouts from another's elemental remains. If we are right in believing that the status of atomistic theories in Ponge's conceptualization of his own writings is a matter of analogical formalism, then a similar relation should hold at the intratextual level too, that is, within the work of Ponge itself. Ponge's writings lead us back through literary history toward original formulations concerning the elements of things and words, and the reader should be able to observe one of his texts depicting its cyclical return to, and development from, its own building blocks.

Michael Riffaterre has stated that a text by Ponge is the formal and semantic development of a kernel-word *(mot-noyau)*, or an elemental complex, such as a phrase or sentence, itself produced by the kernel-word (see Riffaterre 1977, 66 and the introduction to the present work). The cohesion of the Pongian text is, according to this view, correctly explained as dependent

5 / How the Text Rewrites its Atomic Structure

upon the expansion of these basic elements into the integrated whole in which they function. However, this thesis could prove even more useful to an appraisal of Ponge's work if its antithesis were also taken into consideration: at the same time, a text by Ponge hinges upon its reducing itself as a composite body to its own first beginnings.

A good example may be found in Ponge's "Le Carnet du bois de pins" (The notebook of the pine woods), one of several pieces comprising the author's *La Rage de l'expression*. This rather long poem is, as its title suggests, a diaristic work; it was composed during the months of August and September 1940, and its numerous entries are dated, sometimes including references even to time of day (morning, afternoon, evening). The poet's various reflections not only about the pine forest but also the personal language through which he would express it are presented as they were gathered in the notebook over time; they are openly displayed, not as aspects of a creative product but as those of an artistic act that constitutes a poetic parallel to the sometimes constant, sometimes changing aspects of the living woods themselves. That is, instead of offering a vision of the pine forest and of the poem as fixed in time—as would a shorter, polished poem extracted from the poet's sometimes repetitive, sometimes evolving reflections—the diaristic form of the notebook exhibits the mechanisms that produce both it and the poem as living things.

The first part of the text involves defining and describing the pine woods in terms of their composing themselves; indeed, the first title of the piece is "Leur Assemblée" (Their gathering). A number of observations concerning the pine forest and ways of rendering it in language are therefore assembled in the notebook, and we get the sense that one of the things at issue is the poet's sheer delight in the richness of language. Ponge's joy in the word corresponds to the second title, "Le Plaisir des bois de pins" (The pleasure of the pine woods). The evolution of the pine forest as a natural phenomenon is doubled by the various linguistic approaches to its artistic expression. These poetic developments are gathered and assembled by the poet as though to celebrate the analogous processes that he observes within the woods.

Although the emphasis is placed on generation, in the midst of this view there are notes indicating the virtual presence of the dialectical process of degeneration: "Il faut qu'à travers tous ces développements (au fur et à mesure caducs, qu'importe) la hampe du pin persiste et s'aperçoive" [Throughout all these developments (which become deciduous as we go along, but never mind) the stem of the pine must be persistent and perceptible] (*TP,* 331).[1] Even though the pine is not a deciduous tree, but an evergreen, deterioration is central to the pine forest's life; and, in the above quotation, the formal aspect of the sentence reflects this observation by locating the reference to the process of declining ("caducs") in its central parenthesis. Throughout the text, moreover, Ponge reiterates the oxymoronic notion that the pine is the tree "qui fournit (de son vivant) le plus de bois mort" [that supplies (while alive) the most dead wood] (380). Just so, the notebook is the form of writing that produces the greatest amount of "dead wood"; but this rejected material—elements that fall to the ground only to release their vital grains—is in turn reworked into new literary bodies.

For example, "Le Carnet du bois de pins" culminates in its middle section, which is appropriately titled "Formation d'un abcès poétique" (Formation of a poetic abscess); the word *abcès* (abscess), designates localized tissue degeneration and points to the decomposition of the poetic tissue or text. While walking through the woods, one notices that the many individual pines resemble each other very closely, and yet always present certain differentiating features. Ponge renders this observation by incorporating several pages of slightly different variations on the same stanza. The nine lines of these stanzas are built from descriptive words and phrases that have been distilled from the previous part of the text and rearranged in a different poetic form—no longer Ponge's customary prose, but alexandrine verse. The readers move through these eight pages as though they were strolling through the woods, finding a slightly different tree (or stanza) at every turn (of the page). Often titled either "variante" or "autre," each particular stanza imitates an individual tree of the forest. One can get a sense of the passage's cumulative effect by reading two of these sixteen stanzas:

Autre.
L'alpestre brosserie haut touffue de poils verts
Aux manches de bois pourpre entourés de mirrors.
Du corps étincelant sorti de la baignoire
Ou marine ou lacustre au bas-côté fumante,
Sur l'épaisseur au sol élastique et vermeille
Des épingles à cheveux odoriférantes
Secouées là par tant de cimes négligentes,
Il reste un peignoir d'ombre entachée de soleil
Obliquement tissu d'atomes sans sommeil.

❖ ❖ ❖

Autre.
Dans cette brosserie haut touffue de poils verts
Aux manches de bois pourpre entourés de miroirs,
De vous, corps radieux issu de la baignoire
Ou marine ou lacustre au bas-côté fumante,

5 / How the Text Rewrites its Atomic Structure 93

> Il ne reste au tapis élastique et vermeil
> Des épingles à cheveux odoriférantes
> Secouées là par tant de cimes négligentes,
> Qu'un peignoir de pénombre entachée de soleil
> Obliquement tissu d'atomes sans sommeil.
>
> (*TP,* 352–53)

> [*Another.*
> The Alpine brushworks high tufted by green bristles
> With handles of purple wood surrounded by mirrors.
> Of the glistening body come forth from the bath
> Marine or lacustrine whose rim is steaming,
> On the floor's elastic and vermilion thickness
> Of the odoriferous hairpins
> Tossed there by so many negligent treetops,
> There remains a bathrobe of sun-tainted shadow
> Obliquely woven with restless atoms.

❖ ❖ ❖

> *Another.*
> In this brushworks high tufted by green bristles
> With handles of purple wood surrounded by mirrors,
> Of you, radiant body born of the bath
> Marine or lacustrine whose rim is steaming,
> Nothing remains on the elastic and vermilion carpet
> Of the odoriferous hairpins
> Tossed there by so many negligent treetops,
> But a bathrobe of sun-tainted penumbra
> Obliquely woven with restless atoms.]

The difference between the trees is rendered by means of slight changes in the stanzaic lines, that is, following the Lucretian analogy, by simple permutation of textual elements. Then, while expanding Lucretius's letters to entire phrases, Ponge nevertheless reduces his own poem to the following list of distilled, immutable elements:

Voici les éléments indéformables:

1 { Par cette brosserie haut touffue de poils verts
    Aux manches de bois pourpre entourés de miroirs

2 { Du corps étincelant sorti de la baignoire
    Ou marine ou lacustre au bas-côté fumante

5 / How the Text Rewrites its Atomic Structure

3 { Rien ne reste au rapport de mouches sans sommeil
    Sur l'épaisseur au sol élastique et vermeil

4 { Des épingles à cheveux odoriférantes
    Secouées là par tant de cimes négligentes

5 { Qu'un peignoir de pénombre entaché de soleil

(*TP,* 356–57)

[*Here are the immutable elements*:

1 { Throughout this brushworks high tufted by green bristles
    With handles of purple wood surrounded by mirrors

2 { Of the glistening body come forth from the bath
    Marine or lacustrine whose rim is steaming

3 { Nothing remains of the relationship of restless flies
    On the floor's elastic and vermilion thickness

4 { Of the odoriferous hairpins
    Tossed there by so many negligent treetops

5 { But a bathrobe of sun-tainted penumbra]

Immediately following this enumeration, we find the passage quoted below. From the above list nothing remains but the numbers—an even further compression of the lines that compose the variant stanzas:

On pourra dès lors disposer ces éléments *ad libitum* comme suit:
[Consequently, one may arrange these elements *ad libitum* as follows:]

12345	14235
12435	14325
12354	14352
13245	
13542	23451
13425	24351
13254	
13524	23154
13452	etc.

(*TP,* 357)

5 / How the Text Rewrites its Atomic Structure

This is surely one of the strangest passages in Ponge's entire work. One's surprise might be accompanied by the assumption that it is simply some kind of inexplicable, or even mocking, self-parody—a justifiable reaction perhaps, given the title of the next section: "Tout cela n'est pas sérieux" [All that isn't serious] (358). But its very idiosyncrasy may reflect an essential aspect of the entire "Carnet," for even the first lines of the text tell us to read eccentrically:

Leur assemblée   RECTIFIA *ces arbres*
De leur vivant   *à fournir du bois mort*
(327)

We are obliged to read by moving diagonally from line to line, according to the veering arrows: "Leur assemblée à fournir du bois mort de leur vivant RECTIFIA ces arbres" [Their gathering to supply dead wood while alive RECTIFIED these trees]. Therefore, both the beginning of the "Carnet" and the sequence of elements quoted above show that the permutation of textual elements occurs along an oblique axis. This analogically links the poetic reading process to the atomic mechanism of the *clinamen*—the swerving or deviation of the atoms—which, indeed, is illustrated by these columns of shifting numbers.[2] May my own reading and others collide and cohere within a collaborative, poetic whole.

The recomposition of the poetic tissue is therefore left to us, the readers, whose free will is in fact solicited. We are to shift freely the elements constituting the list, as they are shown swerving away from their former positions in the pillars they form. After the permutation of numbers quoted above, the final "etc." sends us back to the words that introduce the sequence: "On pourra dès lors disposer ces éléments *ad libitum* comme suit" [Consequently, one may arrange these elements *ad libitum* as follows]. But there is apparently no end to the sequence, or, if there is an end, it rejoins its own beginning. Cyclical in nature, as is nature itself, the construction demonstrates a poetic principle in Ponge's work: that of the text's coming full circle. The buckled aspect of the text is a "theme" explained by the "phore" with which it is placed in juxtaposition: as atoms and their interminable permutations are to the woods, so the strophic elements and their boundless rearrangements are to the text. By this perpetual combination of numerical elements, the text evokes the woods as "une infinité de colonnes" [an infinity of columns] (337)—a vast, extremely complicated series of shifting atoms. These potentially confusing numerical crisscrosses render not only one's movement through the "labyrinthe" (labyrinth) of the pine forest (337)—whose individual trees are bewilderingly similar—but also the manner in which the pines themselves interweave: "un infini entrecroisement d'aiguilles vertes" [an infinite intertwining of green needles] (339).[3]

But this could have been accomplished by any series of numerical permutations. What can this particular structure tell us about the text's relation to its subject, the woods? Given that Ponge's perspective is atomistic, and that in the "Carnet" he is attempting to reveal the "essential quality" of the woods (361) and their "formula" (339), we may find a connection between the elemental structure of the text and that of the pines in the external world.

Since the stanza consists of nine lines, in the passage of elemental permutations each of the numbers 1 through 4 represents two stanzaic lines (that is, eight lines total). We know this because each individual stanzaic element 1 through 4 is a combination of two lines, as shown in the list of immutable elements by the accompanying brackets. Element number 5, however, represents only a single line. This remaining line is not shown connecting by means of a bracket with another line; it is considered apart, as further indicated by the *ne . . . que* negation (nothing but, only): "3 Rien ne reste au rapport de mouches sans sommeil / . . . / 5 Qu'un peignoir de pénombre entachée de soleil" [3 Nothing remains of the relationship of restless flies / . . . / 5 But a bathrobe of sun-tainted penumbra] (*TP,* 357). Analogically speaking, therefore, elements 1 through 4 are univalent atoms—they form one liaison each. Although there is no indication that element 5 establishes connections, it is in fact tetravalent—it is inextricably linked to the other four stanzaic elements. These bonds are not immediately apparent, but the cohesion of the entire stanza is contingent on element number 5, for there is absolutely no grammatical closure without it. Elements 1 through 4 all tend inevitably toward element 5; without it, they lack structural purpose and meaning.

Just so, deep within the organic molecules that make the woods lies the tetravalent carbon atom; without it, its four univalent units of affinity cannot coalesce.[4] The stanza's numerical structure adequately renders the analogous configuration of carbon composites, and therefore takes us to the very core of the text's subject. But the process of textual appropriateness does not stop here. It sometimes shifts from microscopic to macroscopic levels of the woods, only to return eventually to their first beginnings. Branching out into other parts of the "Carnet," we may observe another remarkable aspect of the text—the way in which it takes a defining geometrical property of the pines into account by drawing our attention to the roughly triangular circumflex accent. Indeed, the circumflex of the word *faîte* (treetop, apex) sits atop an analogical pine, because Ponge reduces this tree to a letter of the alphabet: "Le pin . . . est l'idée élémentaire de l'arbre. C'est un

5 / How the Text Rewrites its Atomic Structure 97

I . . ." [The pine . . . is the elementary idea of the tree. It is an I . . .] (340). Of all the linguistic matter at the poet's disposal, the circumflex best evokes the rudimentary notion of the pine's characteristic figure, and its repetition renders the walker's frequent encounter with this outline, as in this description of the woods:

> Débarassés (jusqu'à la mi-hauteur) de leur branches, à la fois par leur propre souci exclusivement du faîte vert (du cône vert à leur faîte) et par la sérieuse obscurité concertée dans leur foule. . . . (329; emphasis added)
>
> [Relieved (up to midheight) of their branches, at once by their own concern for the green apex exclusively (for the green cone at their apex) and by the serious and concerted obscurity in their midst. . . .]

The circumflex is used with overwhelming insistence throughout the "Carnet"; for instance, the pines are also often called "grands fûts" [tall columns], "grands mâts" [tall masts], etc. Things compared to the pines are therefore not necessarily conical; rather, they are always associated somehow in our mind with a triangle: the *mât* supports the triangular, lateen sail which prevails in the poet's native Mediterranean region; the *fût* bolsters the triangular end of the Greek temple's roof. Even the *cône* is, geometrically speaking, generated by the revolution of a right triangle. This is especially significant, given Ponge's tendency toward etymological motivation, or, as here, remotivation: the pine as a *conifère* (conifer) is redefined in regards to this word's root meaning in Latin, that is, "cone-bearing"; now, in the text, even its cones bear triangles. The triangle is therefore within the cone; it is the cone's "seed."

Let the pinecone drop to the ground, and, after degeneration, out spill its seeds. The text seeks to reveal what is hidden inside—its diminutive form, its "formula": "Pour moi, je suis de plus en plus convaincu que mon affaire est plus scientifique que poétique. Il s'agit d'aboutir à des formules claires. . . ." [In my view, I am becoming more and more convinced that my business is more scientific than poetic. It's a matter of arriving at clear formulas. . . .] (381). In the case of the woods, the core to be discovered is the fundamental, diminutive constituent of wood itself—the minuscule, infinitely repeated triangles of tetrahedral carbon molecules. It is in this central depository of symbolic grains—the container of immortal atomic remains—that each and every one of the transformations leading to the construction of the woods ultimately takes place. Within this chemical composite, the autonomous yet repetitive pine tree and the society of the forest are found, as are the various variants of the strophes composed of permutating elements. It is by visualizing carbon, as the heart of the process of elemental rearrangement within the woods, that we may observe the integration of the repeated, polygonal surface of the mimetic triangular circumflex accents into the singular, polyhedral solid that their joined faces form; for the tetrahedron is to space what the triangle is to a plane:

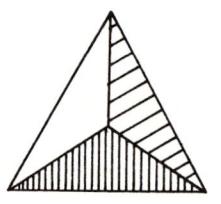

Normally, in such representations, the carbon atom itself is not figured; but it is admittedly present, hidden at the tetrahedron's center of gravity. Enveloping it are its four attractive forces, its four substitutional units of affinity. It is thanks to such carbon composites that all organic compounds, as well as a significant number of inorganic compounds, are produced. (The text itself would vanish if the carbon molecules within the wood from which its pages are fabricated were unraveled.) From no other element, in fact, do substitution compounds arise.

It is owing to the different proportions of these combinatory constituents that each particular tree, like each individual strophe, possesses its specific difference. Each strophe, moreover, is a mirrored image of another strophe: "le bois de pins est entouré de miroirs, de glaces" [the pine woods are surrounded by mirrors, by looking glasses] (*TP,* 358). Our representation of the analogical carbon molecule must therefore be rectified in order to reflect this fact:

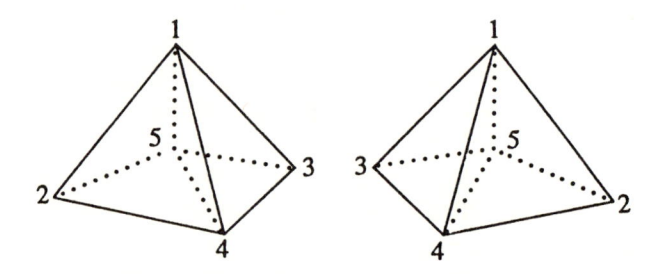

This representation takes into account the notion that these bodies, as shown by Pasteur, possess the power to rotate, as do Ponge's strophes, according to the root meaning of the word itself—a synonym of, or semantic substitution for, "rotation" (Greek *strophe*, "act of turning").[5] Owing to this rotation, the relative position of the four valences of carbon and, analogously, those of the strophe may appear in different arrangements, which allows them to interweave. In this case, the numbers 1, 2, 3 and 4 in our illustration may be relocated at different summits of the tetrahedron. The number 5, however, will always be the only body to remain in the obscure interior, as an axis enveloped by an elementary textile.

We know, furthermore, that the metaphorical body enveloped by the atomic bathrobe of element 5 is that of Venus: "Dans son peignoir, pénombre entachée de soleil, / Sèche aussitôt Vénus sortant de la baignoire" [In her bathrobe, sun-tainted penumbra, / Venus dries immediately while coming out of the bath] (*TP,* 349). Just as in *De rerum natura*, where Venus is, in the beginning at least, reflected in everything, so in Ponge's forest her form and force are everywhere, for the pines are surrounded by mirrors. Presented here, however, is not only the "goddess of traditional religion and mythology" but also "the Empedoclean principle of Love . . . representing the creative forces of the world."[6] Indeed, over the course of several pages in the "Carnet"—the passage where the strophe in question is progressively modified—the evocation of Venus is slowly filtered out, until, at the end of the passage, there is nothing left of her, except the notion of the creative principle's functioning in the world. Yet no longer is this the Empedoclean principle of creation; rather, it is its ethical culmination in the iconoclastic divestment of mythological symbols and the reinvestment of their remains into the doctrines of atomism: "De vous, corps radieux issu de la baignoire / . . . / Il ne reste au tapis élastique et vermeil / . . . / Qu'un peignoir de pénombre entachée de soleil / Obliquement tissu d'atomes sans sommeil" [Of you, radiant body born of the bath / . . . / Nothing remains on the elastic and vermilion carpet / . . . / But a bathrobe of sun-tainted penumbra / Obliquely woven with restless atoms] (353). Just so, in *De rerum natura* (see 1.44–46, 50–57, 62–79), Venus, as the creative force in the world, is soon reduced to the Epicurean theory of the atomic first bodies; for the gods can never intervene in the functioning of the world.

In the woods, atomic generation begins in the naked ovules hidden between, and protected by, the scales of pinecones: "Il revient [aux pins] la fonction de border leur société, d'en cacher les arcanes, d'en cacher le dénuement intérieur. . . ." [The function of hemming their society, of hiding its arcana, of hiding its interior bareness, is the prerogative of {the pines}. . . .] (361). The text aims to uncover these "alchemical" secrets of nature, for they are the true "mothers" of the organic world. Likewise, this text about birth uncovers its own birth in the textual world, and therefore returns to the myth of Venus. But Ponge remotivates the myth; he shows the divinity hidden among the pines, paradoxically wrapped in a materialistic intertexture.

Mythology and science may be seen mixing here: Venus, in her assimilation to Aphrodite, is "the foam risen" (Greek *aphros,* "*foam*"); and science now contends that the life-giving carbon element also originated in the sea. The sea, therefore, according to both ancient mythological and modern scientific explanations, produced the creative forces of nature; it is both *mer* and *mère*. Both Venus and carbon are sea-born, both are, as Ponge's text would have it, "issus de la baignoire" [born of the bath]. But when Empedocles' reduction of Venus had been accomplished, only four combinatory elements remained: earth, water, air, and fire; just as when the lines composing Ponge's strophes are reduced, only four of them are shown combining; just as there are only four elements that, together, compose that substance called "wood": "Le bois est formé [1] de ligno-cellulose . . . , [2] de pentosanes . . . , [3] de cellulose proprement dite et [4] d'hémicellulose. . . ." [Wood is composed of {1} lignocellulose . . . , {2} pentosans . . . , {3} cellulose proper, and {4} hemicellulose. . . .][7] And yet when wood is ultimately reduced, what remains is coal *(le charbon),* whose most important element by far is carbon.

The widespread element of carbon is a Pongian preoccupation that underpins other texts as well. For example, it is an essential piece of Ponge's *Le Grand Recueil: Pièces*: "L'Anthracite ou le charbon par excellence" (Anthracite or coal par excellence] (*GRP*, 71–73), which was written a year later than the "Carnet," that is, in 1941. The centrality of this element pervades even that work whose very title, *Pièces* (Pieces), emphasizes elementariness. In the poem's first lines, the mixing of different linguistic systems—analogous to that accomplished by carbon as it conjoins the various organic systems—may be observed in operation. English and French languages are intertwined here; French imitates English, for, according to the text, it is the latter's soil of origin that has produced the referent:

> Lancashire, tes pelouses grasses retournées — puis longuement encachées *here* — formèrent l'anthracite anglais. (71)

> [Lancashire, your luxurious lawns turned over—then for a long time buried *here*—formed English anthracite.]

The choice of this particular geographical site is significant. *Lancashire*, a metonym for anthracite itself, lies hidden in a phrase to whose centrality point the enveloping dashes that distinguish it as a structural unit:

5 / How the Text Rewrites its Atomic Structure 101

— puis *l*(onguement) ***encach***(é)***es here*** —

The hidden structure of anthracite, which is composed of above 90 percent carbon—making it, indeed, the "charbon par excellence" [coal par excellence] of the subtitle and of the subtext—is "encachée"[buried] *here*, within the form of the text; and yet we, the readers, must, as "chemists," reconstruct its elements into a contiguous formula:

l + *encach* + *es* + *here* = Lancashire.

When somewhat later in the text we read that the third syllable of "anthracite"—"sa dominante" [its dominant]—shines, we are reminded of this mixture of signifying systems, and so see that its brilliance ultimately resides "en cet endroit" [in this place], that is, in the sound of the French word *ci*, the third syllable of the signifier. *Ci* (synonym *ici*, in English, *here*) means "en cet endroit" [in this place]; and thus we are returned to the English word *here* of the text's first lines:

> Certains [des charbons] sont mats. Ignobles en quelque sorte. D'aucuns, par contre, montrent un caractère magnifique. De l'un d'entre eux anthracite est le nom, — dont on voit à la troisième syllabe qu'il brille, si la dernière est tout à fait muette. Sa dominante toutefois brille. Il a en cet endroit quelque chose de réconfortant. A la vue, comme à la prononciation, de tonique. (*GRP*, 71)

> [Some kinds of coal are dull. Somehow vile. Others, on the contrary, display a magnificent temperament. One among them is named *anthracite*—and at the third syllable one sees it shine, while the last syllable is completely mute. In any case, its dominant { = *ci*} shines. It contains something reassuring *in this place* { = Fr. *ci*, *ici*, Eng. *here*}. Something *tonic* with regard to vision as well as pronunciation.] (Emphasis and comments added)

The structure that is hidden in the poem's own form hinges on an imitative reconstruction—in the French language—of the English *Lancashire*, whose *here* is stressed by the text. It is in fact reproduced a second time at this point. Lancashire, the place (the "here" of production), is (metonymically) anthracite, the product. This product, of which the dominant constituent is the element of pure carbon, is itself symbolized by the letter *C*, which, in the English language—imitated by the text—is pronounced very similarly to the third and dominant syllable of the French *anthracite*, that is, *ci*. The "dominante" of the word designating the subject of discourse may be reduced, in this manner, to its "tonique," that is, to its first letter, or first form—the element C, which, in the periodic table of elements, is the metonym (synecdoche) of the word *carbone* (carbon).

That the text advances the idea of resolution is evidenced by the implicit analogical reference to harmonic cadence (that is, chord progression moving to a point of rest). The most widely employed resolution, because the most satisfying—the most *tonique*—is into the tonic, or first tone of the (diatonic) scale used for the musical composition, from the dominant, or fifth note of the scale. Such a process is, of course, more directly evoked, even in the first lines of "L'Anthracite," where there is an allusion to the slow, natural reduction of the primeval forests into coal deposits, now hidden deep within the earth's strata.

And, returning to the "Carnet du bois de pins," this is precisely the natural and poetic mechanism presented in Ponge's text on the forest. As coal is produced by vegetal decomposition, so Ponge's "L'Anthracite" may be said to derive from the dissolution of his "Bois de pins." The literary form of the diaristic notebook, like the woods, results from the ceaseless reformation of the "dead wood" it produces, rectifies, and then reincorporates. Just so, the products of nature constantly return to their first forms, as does everything in its disintegration at death, thereby releasing their elements to be reintegrated into new forms of life.

The reconstructions of nature (and of Ponge or Lucretius) can therefore be more precisely comprehended as a result of the "elasticity" of matter, which Ponge defines in the "Carnet" as follows:

Elastique: qui revient à sa première forme.

(*TP,* 346)

[*Elastic*: that which returns to its first form.]

Perhaps no seme reappears as frequently in the notebook as that of "elasticity" linked to the woods: each of its trees, for example, are "souple comme le caoutchouc" [supple like rubber] (328). Using the "elasticity" of the reed in La Fontaine's "Le Chêne et le roseau" (The oak and the reed), and thus doubling that already implicitly present, on the same page Ponge writes: "*Robuste* revient à une autre sorte d'arbres, mais le pin *l*'est pourtant, bien plus qu'aucun autre il plie et ne rompe pas. . . ." [*Robust* applies to another kind of tree, but nevertheless the pine is *so*, although more than any other it bends and does not break {like the leaning, italicized *l* in Ponge's sentence}. . . .]. *Robuste,* Ponge reiterates, "revient à une autre espèce d'arbres" [applies to another species of tree]; surely, he was thinking of *chêne* (oak), through its etymological connection to *robuste*: Littré notes that this word goes back to the Latin "*robustus, de robus*, archaïque pour *robur*, chêne, force" [*robustus*, from *robus*, archaic for *robur*, oak, force]. On the one hand, this returns us to the place in which words' first forms are conserved— the etymological dictionary. On the other hand, it actually serves to send us back to that first literary form on which the Pongian version proclaims itself based by means of an unreferenced quotation—La Fontaine's famous fable, and its praise of the force of elasticity: "Je plie, et ne romps pas" [I bend, and do not break]. The same verb, *revenir* (to return), in the following quotation serves as a dictionary *renvoi* (cross-reference, literally "sending back") through the web of long, layered definitions presented in the text: "Décidément, il faut que je revienne *au plaisir du bois de pins*" [Indeed, I must return to *the pleasure of the pine woods*] (331); it encourages us to return with the poet to that first attempt at a definition, as announced by the title of a previous section of the text: "LE PLAISIR DU BOIS DE PINS" [THE PLEASURE OF THE PINE WOODS] (327). Thus, through our reading process, we follow in the poet's elastic steps: "Evolutions aisées, parmi tant de colonnes, d'un pas presque élastique, sur ces tapis épais faits d'épingles à cheveux végétales. . . . Et par terre une épaisseur élastique d'épingles à cheveux, soulevée parfois par la curiosité maladive et prudente des champignons" [Flowing movements, among so many columns, with an almost elastic tread, on these thick carpets made of vegetal hairpins. . . . And on the ground an elastic thickness of hair pins, stirred up sometimes by the prudent and morbid curiosity of the mushrooms] (337–38).

"Que le lecteur ici ne passe pas trop vite" [Here, I wish the reader would not go by too quickly]. This list contains a wealth of information to help us move through Ponge's own maze. The last passage cited presents an elaborate overdetermination of the semantic content of *élastique* (elastic).[8] Not only is the word *élastique* applied as an epithet to the dense cover of pine needles on the forest floor, but its semantic network extends to the activity of the mushrooms pushing up through it and stirring it up; for, as we learn in Littré, *élastique* derives from the Greek "*elastes*, le même que *elates* ou *elater*, qui pousse, qui meut, de *elaynein*, pousser, chasser" [*elastes*, the same as *elates* or *elater*, that which pushes, that which moves or propels, from *elaynein*, to push, to chase away].[9] Here, therefore, in Ponge's woods, the sense of *élastique* has swerved from adjectival association with a noun, "épaisseur élastique" [elastic thickness], to its verbal root meaning, "to push" (also, in French, "to grow"). It is linked, moreover, to those growing things, "champignons" [mushrooms], found at the foot of the textual object, that is, at the trees' roots. And at the root of *arbre* (tree), also according to Littré, we find a further semantic association with *élastique* (through the Greek *elastes*): in *arbre* "se trouve un radical *arb* ou *urb*, exprimant ce qui pousse, ce qui est fécond" [one finds a radical *arb* or *urb*, expressing that which pushes {grows}, that which is fruitful]. Hence, we have the root verb *elaynein* pushing its way up through, and next to, nouns, which are also qualified as being elastic. This mixture of dynamism and stasis is evoked to help define the text/object's mode of being: the thing whose action is founded in *elaynein* (to push) acts upon that which is *elastes* (the thing that pushes) in such a way as to make difficult any distinction between verb and noun, because the pushing, elastic mushroom moves up through the moving, elastic forest floor.

The process of attaching the various elements of this complex semantic network to be accomplished by the reader is indicated by the word "épingle" [pin], for it is "that which attaches." And it is used to attach things which are supple, that is, resilient or elastic, like hair, as in the often repeated "épingles à cheveux" [hairpins]. "Cheveux" [hair] conveys both denotations of *élastique (elastes):* "qui pousse" [that which grows] and "qui meut" [that which moves]. Furthermore, since the first sense Littré indicates for the word "épingle" is "petite pointe métallique... dont on se sert généralement pour la toilette" [small, tapered metallic object... generally used as an article of toiletry], we may, in this light, better appreciate Ponge's metaphoric substitution of *épingles* for the characteristic *aiguilles* (pine needles) that fall from "the head" of the trees, "les cimes négligentes" [the negligent treetops] during their "toilette" [grooming]. This metaphor is especially adequate in that it accounts for the formal similarity between real pine needles and hairpins (*épingles à cheveux*), both of which are made of two "branches." And thus, the pun on *pin* (pine tree) in *é-pin-gle* (pin) serves to join the two notions, which are not simultaneously present in the proper French term, *aiguille* (needle).

Indeed, the variant strophes of the "Carnet" consistently present the woods in the ceaseless process, from time immemorial, of making their own toilet: the forest is the "antique brosserie" [ancient brushworks] of Venus who "s'y vint coiffer" [came there to do her hair]. This image also serves to supply a metaphorical link between the object of the text and the text itself: it refers to the process of correcting one's writings, as in the expression "la toilette d'un texte"—the preparation of a manuscript for publication, which the text associates with the natural mechanisms at work in the woods: "Leur assemblée... RECTIFIA ces arbres" [Their gathering ... RECTIFIED these trees]. The text's effort (the effort of *texte*) to return

5 / How the Text Rewrites its Atomic Structure 105

to its own first form is truly elastic: it involves the profusion of a semantic braid that requires a constant return to the level of its roots, its own linguistic *rerum primordia*. In Ponge's woods, it is precisely at the level of the trees' roots—in the carpet of the forest floor—that this ceaseless atomic weaving takes place: "Il ne reste, au tapis élastique et vermeil / . . . / que des rubans tissus d'atomes sans sommeil" [Nothing remains, on the elastic and vermilion carpet / . . . / but ribbons woven with restless atoms] (*TP,* 351). And the text reveals an analogous activity at the root level of the word *text* (Latin *texere,* to weave; *textus,* woven thing, "text"). Inside Venus's bathrobe—her "peignoir de pénombre obliquement tissu d'atomes sans sommeil" [bathrobe of penumbra obliquely woven with restless atoms] considered as a product *(textus)*—lives the ceaseless atomic process of its making *(texere):* "*(Var.)* / Que pénombre habitée d'atomes de soleil / Fréquemment traversée de mouches sans sommeil" [Nothing but penumbra inhabited by atoms of sun / Frequently crossed by restless flies] (354). That is, the exterior limit of the stanza derives from its own interior activity. The "pénombre" of element number 5 is created by the atomic interweaving of the substitutional flies, this activity being reproduced ad infinitum by the surrounding mirrors—for the woods are "entourés de miroirs" [surrounded by mirrors]. Multiplication of the etymological and various semantic registers of *tissu* brings the textual phenomenon full circle: metaphorical atomic weaving *(texere)* produces the text as a woven thing *(textus).* A ceaseless ("sans sommeil") permutation, therefore, between verb and noun is presented; an alternation between the act ("tisser") and the results of the act *(tissu),* presented variously throughout the strophes as "tissus" [fabrics], "rubans" [ribbons], "écharpes" [scarves], "peignoirs" [bathrobes]. The lines' various rearrangements are to the text what the diverse interweavings of atoms are to things.

This infinitesimal mechanism is that of Ponge's text as it permutates its elements. It is the process of a "forme" [form] reverting to its own diminutive, "formule" [formula], or of a "toile" [cloth] becoming a "toilette" [small piece of cloth]. Therefore, on the last pages of the notebook, the forest's cyclical evolution toward decrepitude shows that it, like the text to which Ponge emphatically refers by the diminutive of *opus,* i.e., *opuscule* (a small, minor work), returns to and develops from its own first forms:

```
Un bois de      40 ans se nomme futaie sur taillis
    "      40 à 60      "      "     demi-futaie
    "      60 à 120     "      "     jeune haute futaie
    "      120 à 200    "      "     haute futaie
```

Un bois de plus de 200 ans se nomme haute futaie sur le retour.
Et donc, tout ce petit opuscule n'est qu'(à peine) une "futaie sur taillis." (*TP*, 368–69)

[A forest aged   40 years is called timber over underbrush
   "   40 to 60   "   "   half-timber
   "   60 to 120   "   "   young mature timber
   "   120 to 200 "   "   mature timber
A forest aged more than 200 years is called mature timber on the decline {literally, on the return}.
And so, this entire little opuscule is only (hardly) "timber over underbrush."]

This point of view is especially pertinent to the criticism of Ponge's work because it reveals that his text is a poetic restatement of the nature of things as postulated in Epicurean philosophy. Ponge remotivates that primal analogy formulated in Lucretius's *De rerum natura*, thanks to which the invisible atoms of Epicurus were transformed into readily accessible, poetically manipulatable objects—the elements, or letters of the alphabet. Seen in this light, it does not so much matter whether we describe the text as an expansion or a reduction—as long as we realize that movements in both directions take place, and that neither evolution nor devolution can occur without its dialectical partner. To say that the poem is generated from an elemental core implies, within such an analogical framework, that the text is not a creation ex nihilo; textual assembly is made possible by the deterioration of a composite body and the consequent liberation of its primordial elements. The textual expansion of which Michael Riffaterre speaks is based on what he calls the *mot-noyau*. But this kernel-word has not been created out of nothing. Rather, it is the result of a process that operates continuously on all things—including words and texts as things—reducing complexities into individual constituents. These rudiments are extracted, then recombined into other composites of which they are, to speak like Lucretius, the seeds (see, for instance, *De rerum natura* 1.55–61). Such seeds are indeed echoed in the word *noyau*, which, let us not forget, also refers figuratively to the atomic nucleus, the very core of all things. As nature renews one thing from another, requiring death in order to bring about life, so, according to Ponge, the poetic enterprise is fundamentally re-creative.

Ponge's notion of "text" can be explored in relation to another analogy advanced by Lucretius. According to the ancient Latin poet, the things of the external world, which are formed by the permutations of interlocking atoms, are like woven things. An examination of this primal atomistic comparison, as well as of those already discussed, and the way in which they inform Ponge's poetic practice can sharpen our sense of the poet's understanding and use of analogy in semantic development, especially as it pertains to his place in the history of poetics. Lucretius's analogy, then, will be the subject of the following chapter.

6
Lucretius and the Analogy of Atomic Texture

> La langue est une robe couverte de rapiéçages faits avec sa propre étoffe
> [Language is a robe covered with patches made from its own fabric].
> —Ferdinand de Saussure

Ponge's work refashions its own atomic structure on intratextual, intertextual, thematic, and technical levels. Analogies used by Lucretius in his poetic presentation of Epicurean atomism inform each of these levels, but they have been adapted to the modern poet's purposes. Through this process, Ponge's writings become a homologue of nature, whereby text building and literary history reflect primordial natural mechanisms explained in *De rerum natura*.

Ponge's poetic technique is similar to that of Lucretius: the structure of language—the order of letters, phrases, lines—parallels the structure of the external world as he understands it. Exploitation of the various meanings of words reinforces the correlation; the figurative register of his language often leads us back to etymological roots, thereby suggesting a poetic atomism according to which primal linguistic elements interlace, thanks to the reader's spontaneous movement through the layers of language. In this way, Ponge's reader collaborates by mentally restoring the matter out of which the poet creates his text.

An important aspect of the poet's particular notion of poetry is revealed by the reactivation of an analogical core embedded deep within his language—the semantic nucleus of *text* itself. Ponge's view of art as a homologue of external phenomena is frequently expressed through the analogy between the text and a woven object. For example, in this passage from *Pour un Malherbe*, the poet illustrates his vision of literary history through metaphors that point to the underlying analogy of weaving:

6 / Lucretius and the Analogy of Atomic Texture

[Notre littérature nationale] est composée de nombreux courants qui persistent d'une extrémité à l'autre de son histoire. Au long de cette histoire, des courants se tressent, s'enchevêtrent, courent parfois parallèlement, et ils ne sont pas aisés à débrouiller et à suivre chacun d'un de leurs bouts à l'autre. (*PM*, 162)

[{Our national literature} is made up of numerous trends that persist from one extremity to the other of its history. Throughout this history, trends become braided, become entangled, sometimes run parallel to each other, and it isn't always easy to unravel them and follow each of them from one of their ends to the other.]

And within literary history conceived of as a texture, the same image describes individual texts, such as in the "Argument" of his poem "Le Lézard" (The lizard):

Plusieurs traits caractéristiques de l'objet surgissent d'abord, puis se développent et se tressent selon le mouvement spontané de l'esprit. . . . (*GRP*, 94)

[Several characteristic features of the object spring up first, then are developed and braided according to the spontaneous activity of the mind. . . .]

But perhaps the most interesting thing about the passage quoted above is the analogical link that it establishes between the fabric of the text and the mind. Taking the mind as its model, the text reflects the poet's interwoven intellectual processes.

Ponge often consciously highlights the role he plays in the history of poetics, and his exploitation of this particularly widespread analogy should be understood in historical perspective. For this reason, in this chapter we will explore prior uses of the analogy, reading them in a way that is encouraged by Ponge's own principles of semantic density and textual appropriateness, thereby discovering points of contact with his poetics and, ultimately, with its source in Lucretius. The following chapter will examine more precisely how he rewrites this same basic analogy within the poetic and ethical contexts of his work.

The weaving analogy is fundamental to many figurative references to texts and textual components, and is a common element of texts describing and defining text building. It is especially appropriate in the context of Ponge's project, which is metapoetic and concerned with the banal, the elementary, and the interconnected structure of the world of texts. As various things in the external world share the same kinds of atoms, so different texts share similar analogies, which tie apparently unassociated literary works together in the world of texts.

The textual world is also a world of the mind; and the analogy of interwoven texture pervades different national literatures and historical periods, not only whenever it is a matter of elucidating the nature of the text but also the nature of the intellect. Henry James expresses it metaphorically for the benefit of an aspiring author who is curious about the artist's thought processes:

> Experience is never limited, and it is never complete; it is an immense spiderweb of the finest silken threads suspended in the chamber of consciousness, and catching every air-borne particle in its tissue. It is the very atmosphere of the mind; and when the mind is imaginative . . . it takes to itself the faintest hints of life, it converts the very pulses of the air into revelations. (James 1987, 194)

As discussed in chapter 3, the symbolism of the spiderweb fascinates Ponge, and, like James in the passage just quoted, he evokes it in order to illustrate the act of literary creation.

A related analogy is central to the following passage from Goethe's *Faust*. Like James, Mephistopheles uses the weaving analogy didactically when he speaks to the eager young student (I quote Nerval's translation, since Ponge might well have been familiar with it):

> Il est de fait que la fabrique des pensées est comme un métier de tisserand, où un mouvement du pied agite des milliers de fils, où la navette monte et descend sans cesse, où les fils glissent invisibles, où mille noeuds se forment d'un seul coup. . . . (Goethe 1969, 77–78)

> [It is a fact that the fabrication of thoughts is like a weaver's loom: one movement of the foot sets thousands of threads in motion, the shuttle goes ceaselessly up and down, the threads slide invisibly, and a thousand knots are made with a single stroke.]

Goethe's analogical reference to a loom clarifies the myriad associative bonds that the mind creates spontaneously, while also pointing out that this teeming intellectual activity always extends beyond the confines of strict logical categories.

These remarkable and relatively recent accounts of mental patterns reveal an ancient trope that activates the extensive figurative network associated with the crafts of weaving and sewing. Although used here to describe the structure of the mind, this network also expresses the text in similar terms, and it leads us back through language to its own nuclei.

The analogy of weaving has long been invoked by philosophers and poets alike when describing the skillful use of language and the artistic qualities of texts. For example, the Latin word *filum*, meaning "thread," yet having connotations encompassing anything woven, from linen or woolen cloth to a spiderweb, was used figuratively to designate speech or writing. In this context, *filum* means "texture" or "style," and it appears in this sense in a number of classical writings, such as in Horace's phrase: "tenui deducta poemata filo" [poems so finely spun] (Horace 1926, 414–15).

Concerning ancient Greek literature, the same is true of the word *hyphos*, meaning "(spider)web" or "tissue," and its verbal counterpart, *hyphaino*, "to weave." Longinus, for instance, wrote: "Again inventive skill and the due disposal and marshalling of facts do not show themselves in one or two touches: they gradually emerge from the whole tissue [hyphoys] of the composition...." (Longinus 1953, 124–25).[1] The same comments apply to *rhapsodos*, "person who sews," and the verb *rhaptein*, "to sew." Hesiod, for instance, tells us: "Then first in Delos did I and Homer, singers both, raise our strain—stitching [rhapsantes] song in new hymns [hymnois]" (Hesiod 1929, 280–81). Indeed, as Littré informs us, the word *hymne* itself derives "du lat[in] *hymnus*, qui vient du grec *hymnos*.... D'après Curtius, *hymnos* est de même racine que *hyphao*, tisser, *hyphe*, *hyphos*, tissu; à l'époque reculée où l'écriture était inconnue, la plupart des mots qui servent à indiquer une composition poétique étant empruntés à l'art du tisserand" [from the Latin *hymnus*, which comes from the Greek *hymnos*.... According to Curtius, *hymnos* has the same root as *hyphao*, to weave, *hyphe*, *hyphos*, fabric; in the distant past when writing was unknown, most words used to indicate a poetic composition being borrowed from the art of the weaver].

Much more recently, the eminent French literary analyst, Roland Barthes, has echoed this long tradition by stating that the text is also the Greek word *hyphos*; as he puts it, the text is both "le tissu et la toile d'araignée" [the fabric and the spiderweb] (Barthes 1973, 100–101). Finally, the way in which the modern critic reworks the ancient metaphor corresponds to the picture of poetry and its dissemination that Pindar gave us by saying that the rhapsodes were "the sons of Homer, those singers of deftly woven [rhapton] lays" (Pindar 1957, 328–29).[2] Therefore, the work of the sons is a reweaving of the father's preexistent weaving, a notion that can be applied to Ponge's remotivation of Lucretius.

On the one hand, Ponge's use of the analogy is related to the general history of literature and poetry, but, on the other hand, it is also anchored in the development of the philosophical and literary traditions stemming from Epicurean atomism. Major authors of the Renaissance assured the passage of this tradition into the modern era of French literature. In the following passage, for instance, Montaigne uses an associated metaphor to explain the evolution of atomism, including the Epicurean doctrine of the *clinamen*, or deviation of the atoms, which, as already discussed, is significant in the context of Ponge's poetics:

> [I]l n'estoit pas possible qu'elles se joignissent et se prinsent l'une à l'autre, leur cheute estant ainsi droite et perpendiculaire, et engendrant par tout des lignes parallelles[.] Parquoy, il fut force qu'ils y adjoutassent depuis un mouvement de costé, fortuite, et qu'ils fournissent encore à leurs atomes des queues courbes et crochues, pour les rendre aptes à s'attacher et se coudre. (Montaigne 1978, 1:544)

> [It was not possible for them {the atoms} to join together and coalesce with each other, their fall being so straight and perpendicular, and creating parallel lines everywhere{.} For this reason, therefore, they {the Epicureans} had no choice but to add a fortuitous sideways movement, and, furthermore, they had to give curved and hooked tails to their atoms, so as to make them capable of fastening and sewing themselves together.]

The image evoked by the verb that Montaigne selects, *se coudre* (to sew [each other together]), recalls similar metaphors that he creates in order to describe the act of composing *Les Essais*. For instance, speaking of the quotations that he attaches to his writings, he gives a personal twist to the metaphor, while showing that he causes the borrowed extracts to veer away from their original textual paths so that they become elements of his own text:

> Je tors bien plus volontiers une bonne sentence pour la coudre sur moy, que je ne tors mon fil pour l'aller querir. (1:171)

> [I much more willingly twist good maxims so as to sew them onto myself than I twist the thread of my thought so as to adhere to them.]

In the poetic vein, Ronsard proposes a comparable analogy to illustrate the theme of the emotionally and psychologically interwoven universe of lovers. The following quatrains develop the lyric motif of loving union by referring to Epicurean theories concerning the coherence of external phenomena, particularly the doctrine of the *clinamen*, which allows the atoms to interlace:

6 / Lucretius and the Analogy of Atomic Texture 113

> Les petitz corps, culbutans de travers,
>   Parmi leur cheute en byaiz vagabonde
>   Hurtez ensemble, ont composé le monde,
>   S'entracrochans d'acrochementz divers.
> L'ennuy, le soing, & les pensers ouvers,
>   Chocquans le vain de mon amour profonde,
>   Ont façonné d'une attache féconde,
>   Dedans mon cuoeur l'amoureux univers.
>
> [The little bodies {i.e., the atoms}, tumbling obliquely,
>   During their restless slantwise fall,
>   Knocked together and created the world,
>   Linking together with diverse links.
> Affliction, torment, & avowed feelings,
>   Striking the fruitlessness of my deep love,
>   Have fashioned with a fertile clasp
>   The amorous universe in my heart.]

Later in the same poem, the then prevalent scheme of the microcosm and the macrocosm is illustrated by reference to the natural mechanisms whereby things are perpetually resolved into to their elements, which are subsequently recycled. As the interwoven physical elements are to the world of external phenomena, so the elements of the loved one's body—"tresses" [braids], "doigtz" [fingers], "mains" [hands]—are to the internal world of the poet, and to the poem that will forever embody them and sing their praises in the world of texts:

> Mais s'il avient, que ces tresses orines,
>   Ces doigtz rosins, & ces mains ivoyrines
>   Froyssent ma vie, en quoy retournera
> Ce petit tout? En eau, air, terre, ou flamme?
>   Non, mais en voix qui tousjours de ma dame
>   Par le grand Tout les honneurs sonnera.
>
> (Ronsard 1963, 25)
>
> [But if it happens that these golden braids,
>   These rosy fingers, & these ivory hands
>   Shatter my life, to what will return
> This little whole? To water, air, earth, or flame?
>   No—to a voice whose ceaseless song of my lady
>   Will through the great Whole make her honor known.]

Ponge's conscious connection to ancient tradition, his profound preoccupation with the medium of poetic language, and his positivistic tendencies are aspects of his personality and his work that link him to Epicurus's greatest eulogist, Lucretius. In the Latin poet's work, Ponge finds the most profoundly poetic statements of his kind of artistic love: the appropriateness of text with regard to phenomenal texture, that is, the text as a homologue of its subject. As Lucretius was trying to turn Memmius, for whom his poem was intended, from mythological to materialistic perceptions, the practical problem of clarifying the obscure Epicurean worldview was one of the major concerns. Lucretius's central theme was the ultimate reality of the atoms, but illuminating this arcane subject presented an inevitable obstacle: the atoms are imperceptible. For this reason, in order to illustrate their nature and motions, analogies from the perceptible world were necessary. His solutions are ingenious—simple analogies that bring atomistic theories within the reach of the average mind. So it is in large part through Lucretius's analogies that we learn about atomic mechanisms.

Analogy as such reflects aspects of these mechanisms, for, according to Epicurus, things of the external world constantly produce their own homologues. The vibrating atoms composing objects give rise to very fine atomic films whose configuration is analogous to that of the object from which they emanate. Lucretius calls them *simulacra*, and explains that they cause vision when they come into contact with our eyes. Therefore, things generate representations of themselves, and we know things through these images. Representation to the mind by speech or writing, as Lucretius and Ponge conceive of it, is a *simulacrum* of sorts, in that the text is an analogically formal reproduction of its subject. Therefore, the poet's act is in essence cosmogonic with regard to the textual world, because it is analogous to the processes by which nature produces images of things. The text, which represents things by producing mental images of them, is, in this respect, a homologue of nature, since according to the theory of the *simulacra*, we do not perceive things themselves, but atomic images of things.

For Ponge, this perspective manifests itself not only in literature, but, as our investigation of the poet's assimilation of Rameau's musical theories revealed, in other arts as well. For example, in a text that ostensibly deals with Georges Braque ("Braque ou un méditatif à l'oeuvre"), Ponge refers to the theory of atomic *simulacra* while aligning the painter's artistic point of view with Epicureanism, and therefore with his (Ponge's) own poetics. The passage involves an anecdote that Braque recounted to Ponge. A resident of Sorgues, the town in southern France in which the painter's house was located, told Braque that he was going to send some figs or fish to him as a present. Ponge finishes the story, and comments on it, as follows:

6 / Lucretius and the Analogy of Atomic Texture 115

"Le colis n'arriva jamais, mais cela me parut tout naturel, me dit Braque, et presque *plus* agréable que si je l'avais reçu. Pour ces gens, ce qui a été dit, ou écrit (avec une évidente ferveur), est fait. Nul besoin de le refaire. Et moi, lisant la lettre, moi aussi j'avais savouré, avec quelle joie d'amitié, ces poissons, ou ces figues." Il me semble qu'on pourra juger, par cette déclaration anecdotique du maître sage . . . de la proximité de sa "doctrine" avec celle d'Épicure, notamment à l'endroit où celui-ci expose son hypothèse des *simulacres*, faits d'atomes aussi réels (matériels) que l'objet dont ils émanent. (*AC*, 298)

["The package never arrived, but that seemed perfectly natural to me," Braque told me, "and almost *more* pleasant than if I had received it. For these people, what has been said, or written (with obvious fervor), is finished. No need to do it again. And I, reading the letter, I also had savored, with considerable, friendly joy, those fish, or those figs." I think that one will be able to discern, in this anecdotal declaration of the wise master . . . the closeness of his "doctrine" and that of Epicurus, particularly where the latter presents his hypothesis of the *simulacra* made of atoms just as real (material) as the objects from which they emanate.]

According to Ponge's reading, the anecdote shows that the principles of the painter (an artist working in the realm of visual representation) correspond to the Epicurean notion of the *simulacra*. Paradoxically, in the story, it is not a visual image, or painting, that is like a *simulacrum*, but a text. Moreover, it is Ponge's interpretation of Braque's particular reading of the letter that transforms it from a potential into an actual homologue of the absent objects. Like Braque's still lifes, or Ponge's poetry, the letter embodies the qualities of the figs and fish so powerfully and convincingly, that, to Braque's mind, they appear as real as the real things.

While praising Braque and Epicurus as artistic and philosophical guiding lights—the painter, like the philosopher, is a "maître sage" [wise master]—Ponge refers to the Epicurean doctrine of the *simulacra* in order to explain by analogy that a text can constitute a homologue of a thing, if the material aspect of language, the signifier, is emphasized appropriately. For Ponge, this is equally true of the material basis of all artistic languages. A text or a painting is like an atomic image, because the entire world and each particular thing in it exist by virtue of the rearrangement of shared material elements. An artistic image is therefore every bit as real as the thing it represents. And, according to Ponge, it is this worldview and artistic perspective that Braque's paintings reveal:

6 / Lucretius and the Analogy of Atomic Texture

> Ce que nous donnent à voir les peintures de Braque, ce ne sont que de nouvelles choses (res) qui comportent (car elles sont faites des mêmes "corpores" ou atomes que le monde dit extérieur) l'obscurité et la lumière des choses, qui s'éclairent les unes les autres *(ita res accendent lumina rebus)*. *(AC,* 312–13)
>
> [What Braque's paintings offer to our eyes is nothing but new things (res) that consist of (for they are made of the same "corpores" or atoms as the so-called external world) the obscurity and the light of things, which illuminate each other *(ita res accendent lumina rebus).*][3]

Viewed from this angle, the text is indeed a kind of *simulacrum*. But how does this relate to the analogy of weaving? On many occasions, Ponge has shown that he is very familiar with *De rerum natura*. He would certainly have known that, according to Lucretius, the "textures" of the atomic films impinge on our senses, and that it is therefore thanks to them that the various phenomena of the external world achieve reality in our mind. But in Ponge's references to the tenuous atomic images, the analogy of weaving is as invisible as the *simulacra* themselves, which cannot be seen individually because they mirror their source—the object from which they emanate. This is Ponge's textually appropriate way of leading us back to the intertextual source that his poetics reflects—Lucretius's discussion of the atomic texture of things.

Throughout *De rerum natura*, Lucretius develops an analogy between the intricate network of atoms within external phenomena and the structure of woven things. This widespread analogy overlaps the equally pervasive comparison between atoms and letters at the associated notion of elementariness, an essential and recurrent seme of atomistic metaphors. Working together, these analogies constitute an extended description of the multifaceted texture of the world and of the mind, while also delineating the text on formal, semantic, etymological, and intertextual levels. Among the numerous words whose etymology reveals a prime relation to the creation of sewn and woven objects are the noun *text* and its derivatives. More readily understood today as referring to linguistic phenomena alone, these are words whose figurative impact has become practically imperceptible, as our modern languages have evolved from their ancient sources. For Lucretius and his contemporaries, however, we can suppose that such words were still full of poetic life.

While discussing the cause of vision, Lucretius resumes his previous statements concerning the dissolution at death of body and mind, each returning to its own atoms; then based upon this argument an analogy is

6 / Lucretius and the Analogy of Atomic Texture

drawn, according to which images or films are thrown off from the surface of things, in shape like those things. As revealed by the following quotation, the metaphors employed to extend the analogy often belong to the vocabulary of the textile trade:

> Amongst visible things many throw off bodies, sometimes loosely diffused abroad, as wood throws off smoke and fire heat, sometimes more close-knit and condensed, as often when cicadas drop their neat coats in summer, . . . and also when the slippery serpent casts off his vesture amongst the thorns. . . . There are therefore fixed outlines of shapes and of finest texture which flit about everywhere, but singly and separately cannot be seen. (*De rerum natura* 4.54–69, 87–89)

The phrase *subtili praedita filo* (of finest texture) presents striking references to the guiding metaphor of the passage; for not only the noun *filum* but also the adjective *subtilis* originate—the first more obviously than the second—in the semantic network associated with the weaving art. *Filum* signifies "a thread" and is a metonym of texture. This texture itself is modified by *subtilis*, the etymological signification of which is *sub-tela*. Now *tela* means "web," therefore *subtilis* signifies "finely woven," and then "fine," or "subtle." The passage simultaneously includes an element of a woven thing *(filum)*; compound bodies made of such elements (*tunica*, "coats," in the particular sense, and *vestis*, "vesture," in the general sense); and a reference to the interior structure of these bodies, that is, their context, the way in which their constituents are arranged ("partim diffusa solute . . . partim contexta magis condensaque" [sometimes loosely diffused . . . sometimes more close-knit]).

This linguistic imbrication reveals an intense exploitation of the seme of "wovenness," which reproduces the interwoven structure of the subject of Lucretius's discourse—the intricate texture of the atomic images. The technique is a textual homologue of the mechanism of the *simulacra* themselves, which duplicate the elemental arrangement of the object from which they emanate. It is as though the atomic images were textually appropriate with regard to that object ("ordine eodem . . . subtili praedita filo" [{they have} the same {atomic} order {yet are} endowed with the finest texture]). It is owing to this analogically formal appropriateness within the phenomenal world, according to Lucretius, that we perceive things with accuracy, and our mental images conform to these things' own self-representations, that is, to their *simulacra*.

The human mind responds to the diaphanous textures of the *simulacra* and can combine them into its own images or ideas, because it has an analogous structure; its own fabric is equally rarefied. Indeed, when describing the mind, Lucretius insists on "how fine a texture it is" (*De rerum natura* 3.209). And it is from the contact of these analogous textures that Epicureanism illustrates the link between vision, on the one hand, and thought and dreams, on the other. Their differential quality is located in the relative density of their particular fabric, that of thought and imagination being even more tenuous than that of vision. In fact, the very words employed in reference to the "finely woven" *simulacra* are also used to designate the equally "finely woven" structure of the mind; the external world of things and the internal world of the imagination interlace in language:

> Many images of things are moving about in many ways and in all directions, very thin, which easily unite in the air when they meet, being like spider's web or leaf of gold. . . . Thus it is we see Centaurs. . . . For certainly no image of a Centaur comes from one living, since there never was a living thing of this nature; but when the images of man and horse meet by accident, they easily adhere at once, as I said before, on account of their fine nature and thin texture. [A]ny given one of these fine images easily bestirs our mind by a single impression; for the mind is itself thin and wonderfully easy to move. (*De rerum natura* 4.724–48)

Such linguistic interweaving mirrors the nature of the similar atomic structure of things and human beings. Therefore, whether Lucretius speaks of visible or of invisible, of organic or of inorganic, of animate or of inanimate objects, he readily employs the weaving metaphor. This is so whether the object in question be as dense as iron, described as being braided: "ferrea texta" (6.1054); or as intangible as the very principle of thought and feelings, presented as a web: "quam tenui constet textura . . . animi natura" (3.209–12). And change in phenomena occurs when the atomic texture of one thing comes into contact with the different elemental fabric of another thing:

> [M]any [things] it [i.e., the thunderbolt] transpierces, when the very particles of the thunderbolt have fallen upon the points where the particles of the things are joined in the texture. Furthermore, it easily dissolves bronze and melts gold in a moment, because its mass is made of bodies extremely small and elements all smooth, which easily make their way in, and having so made their way, in a moment loosen all knots apart and slacken all bonds. (6.350–56)

That is, the totality of phenomena—whether the things considered be static or dynamic, palpable or elusive—is accounted for by metaphoric variations of the same analogy:

6 / Lucretius and the Analogy of Atomic Texture

> Observe first of all sea and earth and sky: this threefold nature, these three masses, Memmius, these three forms so different, these three textures so interwoven.... (5.92–95)

The metaphor by analogy employed by Lucretius in order to link the nature of the woven poetic utterance to that of the woven phenomenon of the exterior world is an impetus of Ponge's textual cosmogony. It is marked most emphatically by the following repetition in the first and last books of *De rerum natura*:

> But now to resume my task begun of weaving the web of this discourse. ... (1.418)

> Therefore I will proceed the more readily to weave the web of my discourse. (6.42)

If it is possible to understand Lucretius's "task" as being the source of what we have called Ponge's "linguistic atomism," then we should be able to learn about Ponge not only by reading Ponge, but also by reading Lucretius as Ponge would do. We should be able to observe a similar poetic exploitation of the matter of language, and the creation of a text that is an analogically formal duplicate of its subject—the atomic nature of things, including the mind.

If there is an analogically formal relation between the language of the poet and the external world of phenomena, then, since it is apprehended by the intellect, the text should achieve reality in our mind through the manipulation of the linguistic analogues of atoms, that is, etymological roots. In Lucretius's poem, the verbal root of the "understanding which we call mind and intelligence" (3.139) is employed, as follows, in reference to the godlike Epicurus:

> [W]hen he saw how mortals had ready for them nearly all that need demands for living, and ... [that] nevertheless each had an anxious heart; ... then he understood [intellegit] that the pot itself [i.e., the mind] made the flaw.... (6.9–17)

As a pot contains assorted flavors and aromas that intermingle in it, so the human mind brings together and joins the various phenomena of the external world in its own fabric. However, this process is impeded, as the above passage later points out, when the pot is riddled with holes (an allusion to the urn of the Danaids)—holes of discontent and metaphysical anxiety that Epicurus's philosophy can fill. The nature of the truly Epicurean intellect is revealed by the linguistic roots that express it: the Latin verb *intellego* [*inter* + *lego*], "to see into, perceive, understand," derives from the verb *lego*, "to bring together, to gather, collect." Some etymologists refer *lego* to the root *lig-*, "to tie," and several dictionaries list *intelligo* as a synonym of *intellego*.[4] What is brought together here, as we learn from *lego*'s etymology, can be textile material in the formation of thread, whose function is to tie; for in poetic usage, as Ernout and Meillet note (1959), the verb signifies to spin (thread): "*legere fila* 'filer'."[5] Following this reasoning, *inte(r)-legere* is the capacity of the mind to bring together, and bind these various elements (the process of *texere*), thereby making a texture (the product, *textus*)—a process and a product analogous to those composing the atomic texture of the world.

The act of reading duplicates this activity: *lego* also signifies "to read." All literary—indeed, all linguistic activity—is recuperated here, inasmuch as *lego* derives from the Greek *lego*, whose verbal noun is *logos*. This word itself gathers and joins together every meaning relative to language, be it verbal (including written) expression in the general or in the particular sense, the thing spoken of, computation and reckoning, or the Word as the agent in the world's creation.

And yet this is still an unsatisfactory summary of the semantic network of *lego*; for it also signifies *choice* (that is, free will). According to Ernout and Meillet, *intellego*, the power of the mind, means "choisir entre (par l'esprit), d'où 'comprendre, connaître, s'apercevoir'" [to choose between (with the intellect), whence "to understand, to know, to realize"]. As Lucretius expresses it: "The rest of the spirit . . . obeys and is moved according to the will and working of the intelligence" (*De rerum natura* 3.143–44). Hence the mind itself is analogous to the texture of things according to Epicurean physics. For the gathering of elements that produces a thing results from the swerve of the autonomous atom; likewise, it is owing to our own free will that we may gather together the various elements of language, and thereby participate in the *logos*. Demonstrating this is yet another meaning of *lego*: "to make one's way over, traverse"; *uestigia legere*, to follow the track (of)" *(Oxford Latin Dictionary)*. The way to cross over into that ultimate, godlike contentment (ataraxia), the ethical goal of Epicureanism, is therefore the power of the intellect as discovered in the semantic web surrounding its very name, and whose sometimes swerving threads we, readers of poetry, may choose to follow.

Analogy itself is a primordial element of thought processes, and it underlies the figurative use of language that abounds in poetry. Ponge's work develops from this irreducible element of poetic construction and acknowledges its own formal, semantic, and intertextual first beginnings. Our analyses of Ponge's writings frequently revert to the analogical model, because it provides a foundation for their diverse metaphorical components. Analogy is to poetry what the infinitesimal atomic nucleus is to all phenomenal intertwinings—around it revolve the interrelating associations with which the poetic world is built.

The word *valence* indicates the capacity of an atom to form interatomic bonds, that is, to interlace with other atoms; and one can describe Ponge's poetry as a polyvalence of metaphors of textual construction gathered together thanks to the spontaneous movements of the reader's mind. These metaphors interlace through the model syntagm of analogy, and stretch toward semantic infinity. But as they expand elastically, like things in the external world, Ponge's metaphors also return to the primal analogical cores that provide their basis.

Ponge's use of analogy is conditioned by the functioning of the exterior world of the atoms according to Epicurean physics and its poetic development in *De rerum natura*. It is with the extratextual world that the textual world must ultimately overlap in the poetic process of appropriateness. How better to interlace word and world than by means of the repetitive, parallel pattern provided by the model of proportion (the "warp"), combined with metaphoric rearrangements of it (the crossing threads of an imaginative "woof")? The vast number of thematic variants produced in this way adequately parallels, in the texture of words, the variety of things in the texture of the world. And this coinciding poetic texture becomes denser still when filled with metaphors of interweaving and text(ure).

The definition of world, mind, and words as fabrics leads to Ponge's ethical goal of cleansing them. We will discuss this aspect of the poet's work in the following chapter.

7
Cleansing the Textures

> Mais nous devons, pour exprimer notre sensibilité au monde extérieur, employer ces expressions qui sont souillées par un usage immémorial. . . . [But we must, to express our sensitivity to the external world, utilize these expressions that have been sullied by an immemorial usage. . . .].
>
> —Ponge, "La Pratique de la littérature"

> Telles paroles, telles moeurs, ô société! Tout n'est que paroles [As words, so morals, o society! All is but words].
>
> —Ponge, "Des Raisons d'écrire"

Expanding Lucretius's metaphor discussed in the previous chapter, Francis Ponge often either implicitly or explicitly remotivates his poetic compositions as weaving. Relying on this conceptualization of his writings, we can conjoin various registers of figurative language, thereby bringing our reading to bear on the poet's semantic notion of "text" and reconstructing his harmonious vision of Word and World.

In the earliest poem published as part of his work, Ponge assimilates the text to a fabric. The piece begins as follows:

> O draperies des mots, assemblages de l'art littéraire. . . .
> ("La Promenade dans nos serres," *Proêmes*, in *TP*, 145)[1]
>
> [O draperies of words, assemblies of literary art. . . .]

Variations of this metaphor, despite—or, rather, because of—their banality, pervade Ponge's entire work. Another critic has apologized for his own use of the banal metaphor of weaving in his discussion of Ponge's poetry (see Aron 1980, 70). I do not feel so obliged, because it is not only a question of applying this metaphor to Ponge's writings but also of discovering its role therein. As discussed in the previous chapter, the very fact that, long before his time, the image in question had already become a poetic and metapoetic commonplace makes it an appropriate part of his atomic poetics, which extols base elements and the composite bodies formed by their natural or artistic rearrangements.

Things that are banal preoccupy Ponge, for our point of equilibrium, our very salvation, is to be found in them. In his work, the things nearest to us—those that we ordinarily take for granted and utilize most indifferently—are the things that support our existence. They are the stepping-stones of an epistemology (from the Greek *epistanai*, "to stand upon"). As Ponge puts it: "Que fait un homme qui arrive au bord du précipice, qui a le vertige? Instinctivement, il regarde au plus près. . . . On porte son regard à la marche immédiate. . . ." [When he arrives at the edge of the abyss, and is overcome by vertigo, what does a man do? Instinctively, he looks at the nearest thing. . . . One directs one's gaze to the nearest step. . . .] ("Tentative orale," in *GRM*, 246).

They are also the handrails of an ethics: "L'homme qui vit ce moment-là, il ne fera pas de philosophie de la chute ou du désespoir" [The man who experiences that moment won't invent a philosophy of downfall or of despair] (ibid.).[2] Elsewhere, for example, while suggesting his difference from other poets, Ponge links the commonplace objects that we take for granted and the hackneyed comparisons that invoke them:

> On vous dit: "Vous avez le coeur dur comme une pierre." Or les pierres, c'est autre chose, elles ont peut-être le coeur dur, mais aussi d'autres qualités. Mais on entend une fois pour toutes "les pierres sont dures." C'est fini. C'est fini, on n'en parle plus. Les autres qualités, non. C'est dur. C'est, somme toute, constamment comme moyen, moyen terme d'homme à homme qu'on s'occupe des choses, jamais pour elles-mêmes. ("La Pratique de la littérature," in *GRM*, 270–71)

> [You are told: "Your heart is as hard as stone." Now stones, that's something else, perhaps they have a hard heart, but other qualities as well. But you hear once and for all "stones are hard." It's over. It's over, nothing more to talk about. The other qualities, no. It's hard. It is, in a word, constantly as a means, a middle course between humans, that we consider things, never for themselves.]

Indifference is being attacked here; in its stead we find its antithesis: personal bias, *le parti pris*.

Ponge's project of rehabilitating what he considers to be the unhealthy disregard for the poetic potential of common objects may be perceived in a number of his writings where the "simple things" in which he is interested, with which and against which he works, are, analogously, also words and their fabrics and the "dirt" that has collected on them:

> Si j'ai choisi d'écrire ce que j'écris, c'est aussi contre la parole.... Et souvent, après une conversation, des paroles, j'ai l'impression de saleté. ... Ce n'est pas propre. Et mon goût pour l'écriture c'est souvent, rentrant chez moi après une conversation où j'avais eu l'impression de prendre de vieux vêtements, de vieilles chemises dans une malle pour les mettre dans une autre malle, tout ça au grenier, vous savez, et beaucoup de poussière, beaucoup de saleté, un peu transpirant et sale, mal dans ma peau. Je vois la page blanche et je me dis: "Avec un peu d'attention, je peux, peut-être, écrire quelque chose de propre, de net." (Ibid., 266)

> [If I have chosen to write what I write, it's also against speech.... And often, after a conversation, an exchange of words, I have the impression of dirtiness.... It's not clean. And my appreciation of writing is often such that, returning home after a conversation during which I had felt as though I were taking old clothes, old shirts from a trunk to put them in another trunk, all that in the attic, you know, and lots of dust, lots of dirt, I feel somewhat sweaty and dirty, uncomfortable with myself. I see the white page and I say to myself: "With a little care, I can, perhaps, write something clean and neat."]

Not only are words tissues, but tissues enveloping our own bodily tissues; the state of affairs of the former is therefore in direct proportion to, "rubs off onto," that of the latter. The maintenance of the one is, in this sense, equivalent to the care of the other, and this concern constitutes not only an artistic but also a moral duty. The realms of the artistic and of the ethical are as intimately fused as are our epidermis and the clothing of language.

Metaphors, considered as objects, are naturally part of the material to be remodeled or cleansed by the ethically minded poet-artisan. He expresses this in the following passage of a book appropriately titled *Le Savon*, where the nouns *le pain* (bread), *le savon* (soap), and *l'électricité* (electricity) are also the titles of three texts by Ponge, including the one we are reading:

> [P]armi les objets de fabrication humaine les plus courants, indispensables, ... parmi ceux qu'on utilise ordinairement sans s'en rendre compte, comme Monsieur Jourdain faisait de la prose, se trouvent—aussi bien que le pain, le savon ou l'électricité—les mots et les figures de langage: il apparaîtra aussitôt que les véritables fabricants (et non les simples contemplateurs) de ces objets-là sont les écrivains, les poètes.... (*S,* 125)

7 / Cleansing the Textures

[Among the commonest, indispensable objects of human creation, . . . among those that one uses without ordinarily being conscious of it, as Monsieur Jourdain used prose, are—as well as bread, soap, or electricity—words and figures of speech: it will be apparent immediately that the true creators (and not the mere contemplators) of such objects are writers, poets. . . .]

The fusion of opposing semantic realms is threaded throughout the text; for Monsieur Jourdain is the oxymoronic *Bourgeois Gentilhomme* (Bourgeois aristocrat) to whom the widespread antinomy between prose and poetry must be explained. And yet it is precisely this hackneyed distinction between *prose* and *poème* that Ponge rejects in order to gather the elements together, stitching them into a fluid oneness at those points where they form common se(a)m(e)s.

Thus we have the very title of a Pongian work that is formally similar, in its antilogic, to Molière's: *Proêmes* ("prose" + "poèmes"). This title word also evokes the intertext of Lucretius' own proems to books 1, 3, 5, and 6 of *De rerum natura*, where the god-like *man*, Epicurus, is acclaimed. Such imbrication in Ponge's work says something relatively simple, yet of great ethical (fablelike) significance: it is from the simplest, most apparently prosaic phenomena, preexistent in the nature of things and of language—in language as a homologue of nature—that ultimately emanate even the most gloriously complex poetic constructions, gathered together by, and for the enjoyment of, the human intelligence.

Upon investigation of the repeated, analogical presentation of linguistic constructions as woven tissues, we find new metaphors inserted within the same basic proportion. For example, in an early piece, "Des Raisons d'écrire" (1929–30), while discussing the need for the development of a new rhetoric, Ponge speaks of the words he must use in his poetry:

Un tas de vieux chiffons pas à prendre avec des pincettes, voilà ce qu'on nous offre à remuer, à secouer, à changer de place. (Proêmes, in TP, 185)

[A heap of filthy dirty old rags, that's what we've been given to shift, shake, and move about.]

Now, there is hardly a more insipid tissue than a *chiffon* (rag): "morceau de quelque vieille étoffe" [piece of some old fabric], according to Littré. Yet due precisely to its common nature, its incorporation into Ponge's project is accomplished with ease, without disturbing the larger and anything but banal tapestry of his poetry.

7 / Cleansing the Textures

Insofar as it suggests a required cleansing, the above quotation from *Proêmes* also brings to the fore what we may call the "hygienic" aspect of Ponge's work. The poet has expressed the same notion in several texts, such as in this passage from *Le Savon*:

> Violente envie de faire toilette.
> Cher lecteur, je suppose que tu as parfois envie de faire toilette?
> Pour ta toilette intellectuelle, lecteur, voici un texte sur le savon.
> (*S*, 29–30)

> [Violent desire to have a wash.
> Dear reader, I suppose that you sometimes feel like having a wash?
> For your intellectual hygiene, reader, here's a text about soap.]

The word *toilette*, as discussed in chapter 5, functions both implicitly and explicitly in both its common and etymological meanings in different places throughout Ponge's writings. Indeed, a fusion of these various semantic strata is revealed by comparing different appearances of the word. For example, with regard to the spiderweb and its varieties, and invoking the metaphor of the poetic "wind" that shapes these text(ure)s, Ponge writes:

> Selon les cas et les espèces — et la puissance d'ailleurs du vent —,
> Il en résulte:
> Soit de fines voilures verticales, sorte de brise-bise fort tendus,
> Soit des voilettes d'automobilistes comme aux temps héroïques du sport,
> Soit des toilettes de brocanteurs,
> Soit encore des hamacs ou linceuls assez pareils à ceux des mises au tombeau classiques.
> ("La Nouvelle Araignée," in *GRP*, 199)

> [According to the situation and the species—and, moreover, the strength of the wind—
> The result is:
> Either thin, vertical sails, a kind of very taut half-curtain,
> Or motorists' veils as during the heroic days of the sport,
> Or the doilies of antique dealers,
> Or even hammocks or shrouds fairly similar to those of classical entombments.]

These "linceuls assez pareils à ceux des mises au tombeau classiques" [shrouds fairly similar to those of classical entombments], besides being

7 / Cleansing the Textures   127

the winding sheets of the spider's preys, also constitute an intertextual thread that has to do with thread itself: the interminable weaving of Laërtes' shroud, woven during the day and yet unraveled secretly each night by Penelope in Homer's *Odyssey*. The allusion continues here, clarifying the analogy between the shroud and the *métaphore filée* (threaded metaphor) of the spider's little cloth *(toilette):*

> L'araignée, constamment à sa toilette
> Assassine et funèbre,
> La fait dans les coins;
> Ne la quittant que la nuit. . . .
> ("La Nouvelle Araignée," in *GRP*, 200)

> [The spider, constantly at its little cloth,
> Fatal and funereal,
> Makes it in the corners;
> Leaving it only at night. . . .]

Having been promised an answer upon the termination of this "web," Penelope's suitors waited leisurely, like spiders in their hammocks, until, like the spider's preys in their woven shrouds, they finally met with their own death, at the end of the poem (of the *textus*), upon Odysseus's return:

> Là-dessus elle agit en funambule funeste:
> Seule d'ailleurs, il faut le dire, à nouer en une ces deux notions,
> Dont la première sort de corde tandis que l'autre, évoquant les funérailles, signifie souillé par la mort.
> (Ibid., 199)

> [Thereupon it acts like a funereal funambulist:
> Alone, it must be said, to knot these two notions into one,
> The first of which comes from cord whereas the other, evoking funeral rites, signifies sullied by death.]

Once again we see the continual rewriting of the text, as its present rejoins its past, from which its discourse is separated by centuries: the fusion of that first weaver of poetry, Homer, with the arachnean rhapsode, Ponge. The revivification of such an ancient topic in the work of the modern poet is yet another aspect of the hygienic principle: it is the baptismal, resurrectional link between things old and new, revealed by the separation of fused word-tissues, as the historically rich seme of wovenness returns elastically to its first linguistic form:

> [L]a mémoire sensible est aussi cause de la raison,
> Et c'est ainsi que, de *funus* à *funis*,
> Il faut remonter,
> A partir de cet amalgame,
> Jusqu'à la cause première.
>
> Mais une raison qui ne lâcherait pas en route le sensible,
> Ne serait-ce pas cela, la poésie:
>
> Une sorte de *syl-lab-logisme*?
> Résumons-nous.
>
> (Ibid., 199–200)
>
> [Sentient memory is also the cause of reason,
> And hence from *funus* to *funis*
> We must climb back up,
> Starting from this mixture,
> To the first cause.
>
> But a reasoning that wouldn't drop the perceptible along the way,
> Might that not be poetry:
>
> A kind of *syl-lab-logism*?
> Let's summarize.]

Here again, taken up to be reworked, is the intertext of Penelope's "pretext." For Penelope adopts, as a pretext, her weaving of the shroud, and she, like the spider, "revient plusieurs fois . . . à son point de départ" [returns several times . . . to its point of departure] (ibid., 127) until, in the end, the shroud supposedly meant for Laërtes becomes instead the web in which her suitors, who hang in the balance, are trapped and destroyed. Just so, we, the readers, hang on the words of the Pongian spider and are ultimately enveloped by a diminutive text within a text, a *toilette* within a *toile*. We are trapped in the prey's shroudlike cocoon, of which the spider's web will be "cleansed" at feeding time, thus providing nourishment to the weaver, just as Odysseus's estate takes on new vigor as it gets rid of the defamatory hangers-on.

Ponge has appropriated another woven object that traps as a metaphor of the text. Its special texture is spongelike, and it is not the readers this time, but the poet himself, who has been sucked up by the noun that designates the fabric—phonetically, *serviette-éponge* (terry-cloth towel) sounds like *serviette et Ponge* (towel and Ponge):

Chère serviette-éponge, ta poésie ne m'est pas plus cachée que celle de tout autre objet aussi habituel ou plus rare.
("La Serviette-éponge," in *NNR*, 1:25)

[Dear terry-cloth towel, your poetry is no more hidden from me than that of any other object as common or rarer.]

Here, the fabric and the fabricator are as inseparable as the spider and its web, about which the poet declared: "il est sensible . . . que l'araignée avec sa toile ne fasse qu'un" [it is evident . . . that the spider with its web make one] ("La Nouvelle Araignée," in *GRP*, 197). The one soaks up the other in the playful onomastics of the bathroom.[3]

In Ponge's writings, the word and the notion *toilette* are associated with both the seme of "wovenness" and that of "cleanliness." *Toilette* derives from *toile* (Latin *tela*, web, from *texere*, to weave, whence *textus*, woven thing, "text"), of which it is the diminutive: *petite toile* (e.g., *chiffon*). The little tissues that are words are in need of washing *(toilette);* for, as we read in "Des Raisons d'écrire":

N'en déplaise aux *paroles* elles-mêmes, *étant données les habitudes que dans tant de bouches infectes elles ont contractées*, il faut un certain courage pour se décider non seulement à écrire mais même à parler. (*TP*, 185)

[With all due respect to *words* themselves, *given the habits that in so many filthy mouths they* {"words," also called, as we have seen, "filthy dirty old rags," i.e., "dirty little cloths"} *have contracted*, one needs a certain amount of courage to decide not only to write, but even to speak.]

A certain tautology appears here, according to which we may formulate the following: "les toilettes ont besoin qu'on leur fasse la toilette afin qu'elles puissent ensuite elles-mêmes se faire et puis nous faire la toilette" [the little cloths need us to wash them so that afterwards they may become able to wash themselves and then wash us]. It is only after, or at least during, such a process that from these clean, elemental *toilettes* a pure, composite *toile* may be made. That this process is of importance in the work of Ponge is manifest in the sarcasm of the following passage:

Le chic serait de ne faire que des "petits écrits" ou "Sapates" mais tels qu'ils tiennent, satisfassent et en même temps reposent, lavent après lecture des grrrands métaphysicoliciens. (*Proêmes*, in *TP*, 220)

[It would be great to produce only "little writings" {i.e., "little texts, little fabrics, diminutive cloths"} or "Sapates" {i.e., a considerable present hidden in another one that is comparatively negligible—Littré gives the example of a lemon with a big diamond inside}, but such that they hold up, satisfy, and at the same time relieve, wash {i.e., wash us} after reading the gr-r-r-eat metaphysicolicians.]

This passage once again associates the hygienic principle with the fusion of opposing semantic elements, as we learn from Littré's definition of the term that Ponge chooses for his writings: "SAPATE, s.m. Présent considérable sous la forme d'un autre qui l'est beaucoup moins, un citron par exemple, et il y a dedans un gros diamant. . . ." [SAPATE, s.m. A significant gift in the form of another, much less significant one—a lemon, for instance, with a big diamond inside. . . .]. The seme of "banality" (e.g., a lemon) and that of a contained "preciousness" (e.g., a diamond) combine to create the fused entity, the analogical sum of which is Ponge's own preciosity and the valuable moral lessons of his writings that concern the apparently insignificant.

Nature too performs its own *toilette*, of which the Pongian text has sponged up the essential, metaphorical juice, transferring it from the natural to the artistic textual process. "L'Insignifiant," the first poem of Ponge's collection, *Pièces*, is revealing when studied in this context:

L'INSIGNIFIANT
"Qu'y a-t-il de plus engageant que l'azur si ce n'est un nuage, à la clarté docile?
Voilà pourquoi j'aime mieux que le silence une théorie quelconque, et plus encore qu'une page blanche un écrit quand il passe pour insignifiant.
C'est tout mon exercice, et mon soupir hygiénique." (*GRP*, 7; this is the entire text)

[THE INSIGNIFICANT
"What is more engaging than the azure sky if not a cloud of docile clarity?
That is why I prefer any theory at all to silence, and even more than a blank page, a text when it passes for insignificant.
It is my entire exercise, and my hygienic sigh."]

Two striking words in this very brief text are *nuage* (cloud) and *hygiénique* (hygienic). The word *hygiénique* establishes intratextual links that at once refer to and extend *Pièces*: our reception of the elemental notion of hygiene is tempered by other texts by Ponge. Relating *hygiénique* only to the passages already cited from other works will reveal some very significant networking. And the network extends further still when we observe that *nuage*, to which *hygiénique* is implicitly joined, owing to the cloud's production of (cleansing) rain, is colored by the use of related words throughout Ponge's writings. On the intertextual level, Ponge is certainly invoking all the clouds of romantic poetry; but on the intratextual level, as we read on in *Pièces* and elsewhere in his work, it becomes apparent that clouds themselves are presented as textile products, as in this passage from "Le Pigeon" (The pigeon):

> Puis envole-toi obliquement, parmi un grand éclat d'ailes, qui tirent, plissent ou déchirent la couverture de soie des nues. (*GRP*, 9)
>
> [Then fly away obliquely, in a great flash of wings, which stretch, pleat, or tear the silk blanket of clouds.]

But clouds are not always the same kind of fabric, nor do they always serve the same purpose. Clouds are also a great cleaning cloth ("torchon"), and, as such, they maintain the hygienic state of nature, *ils font la toilette* (they wash). Here, they soak up atmospheric moisture, and, when saturated, implicitly drip it on the earth below:

> Du grand baril des cieux, c'est la bonde radieuse, souvent enveloppée d'un torchon de ternes nuées, mais toujours humide, tant la pression du liquide intérieur est forte, tant sa nature est imprégnante. ("Le Soleil placé en abîme," in *GRP*, 159)
>
> [Of the great barrel of the skies, it is the radiant plug, often enveloped by a cleaning cloth of drab clouds, but always humid, so great is the pressure exerted by the liquid within, so impregnating is its nature.]

Such cloud-cloths have many uses. But they must be moved over, rubbed against, wrapped around the things that they dust, polish, wipe, or absorb. What activates them? We can respond by returning to "L'Insignifiant," where we explore the word *soupir*, which *hygiénique* modifies. We find that the etymology of *soupir* leads us back to the Latin verb *spirare*, to breathe (out), to aspire to, which, in French, gives *souffler*, carrying with it a connotation of (suggestive) speech. It is this emotional breath (*soupir*), then, that is cleansing and health-restoring—"soupir hygiénique" [hygienic sigh].

Breath as a creative principle, a traditional image of poetic inspiration, has long been metaphorically associated in literature with wind. Indeed, we find this very connection in "L'Insignifiant" with the word *soupir*— according to Littré: "*suspirare*, de *susum*, en haut, et *spirare*, souffler" (*suspirare*, from *susum*, above, and *spirare*, to blow)—the wind that moves the cloud across the sky above, and at the top of the first page of *Pièces*. The cloud, as a fabric-word, is, according to Ponge's metapoetic statements, in need of cleansing, and it is described as being yielding ("nuage à la clarté docile"). *Docile*, in its connotation of "capable of being remodeled"—Littré notes that "Il se dit . . . des choses qui se prêtent, qui obéissent" [It is said . . . of things that lend themselves to something, that obey]—allows us to envisage not only the wind's role in the reforming of cloud masses but also the poet's breath ("*mon* soupir hygiénique") as the agent of the suggested refabrication of the intimate, interior texture of words:

> Une fois, si les objets perdent pour vous leur goût, observez alors, de parti pris, les insidieuses modifications apportées à leur surface par les sensationnels événements de la lumière et du vent selon la fuite des nuages, . . . ces continuels frémissements de nappes, ces vibrations, ces buées, ces haleines, ces jeux de souffles, de pets légers.
> . . . Et suivant les volontés ou caprices de quelque puissant souffleur en scène, ou peut-être les coups de vent, ceux que l'on sent aux joues et ceux que l'on ne sent pas, elles [ces milliers d'ampoules ou fioles suspendues à un firmament] s'éteignent ou se rallument, et revêtent le spectateur en même temps que le spectacle de robes changeantes selon l'heure et le lieu. ("La Robe des choses," *GRP*, 8–9)

> [If ever you should lose interest in objects, then observe, with bias, the insidious modifications brought to their surfaces by the sensational events of the light and the sky depending on the swift passage of the clouds, . . . these continuous quiverings of sheets, these vibrations, these condensations, these breaths, these games of gusts, of slight puffs.
> . . . And according to the will or whim of some powerful theater prompter, or perhaps the blasts of wind, those that one feels on one's cheeks and those that one doesn't feel, they {these thousands of bulbs or flasks suspended in the firmament (i.e., the words on the page)} are extinguished or light up again, and cover the spectator {the reader} at the same time as the show {the text} with changing robes according to the time and the place.]

Given the use of the word *spectacle* (show) here, we associate this passage's *souffleur en scène* (theater prompter)—literally, "blower"—with a *metteur en scène* (theater director), that is, one who assembles various parts (roles, scenes) into a composite whole (a show). These overtones reinforce the notion that the poet's, or other artist's, craft (in the sense of *métier*, both "craft" and "loom") is "l'art des permutations" [the art of permutations] ("Braque ou un méditatif à l'oeuvre," in *AC*, 314). That is, the poet continually recasts the elements of language—*les remettant*, as the idiom would have it, *sur le métier* (literally, putting them back on the loom). Just so, the wind blows clouds into the spectacular arrangements that delight us, for they put things in a new light.

The reconstruction of the cloud's *clarté* (clarity)/texture (and that of all word-fabrics) is linked to the linguistic act of the textual voice, *quelque puissant souffleur en scène* (some powerful theater prompter), and its motivating breath is assimilated to a meteorological phenomenon, *les coups de vent* (blasts of wind), as indicated here by clouds moving toward the reader:

> D'Ouest viennent par rafales les gros soucis, les rembrunissements bleuâtres (chargeant (occupant) d'un décor mouvementé) tout le haut (les deux tiers supérieurs) de la page, et parfois la trempant toute entière, mouillant, aspergeant parfois jusqu'au lecteur (dans le cadre de sa fenêtre).
> (Tout l'espace entre le lecteur et la page traversé d'ailleurs par le vent (plein flux) de plein fouet[.]) (*N*, 68)[4]

> [From the west {i.e., from the left in relation to the page viewed as a kind of meteorological map across which words move} come in gusts the serious concerns, the bluish overcasts (filling (occupying) with a stormy setting) the whole top (the upper two-thirds) of the page, and at times drenching it entirely, soaking, spraying at times even the readers (within the framework of their window).
> (The whole space between the readers and the page traversed moreover by the wind (intense flow) with uncontrolled whipping force{.})]

Thus the poet's breath is a truly re-creative force. It reforms and cleanses a banal poetic image: the cloud regains the status of dignity, and even supersedes a symbolic, celestial rival: "Qu'y a-t-il de plus engageant que l'azur si ce n'est un nuage, à la clarté docile?" [What is more engaging than the azure sky if not a cloud of docile clarity?] ("L'Insignifiant," in *GRP*, 7).

For Ponge, there is nothing more fascinating or significant than what seems to be insignificant. The poet prefers *un nuage* to *l'azur* because, in the lyric-poetic and absurdist traditions that he dismisses, this symbolic sky is associated with a nostalgia that unhygienically removes us from our nearby environment. Rather than wishing to escape from this world in order to travel to a place beyond, the poetic process concentrates on the artisan's repair of the elements of our immediate surroundings. Instead of dreaming of a remote paradise, the poet perceives its virtual existence here, in our midst:

> Ici, tout n'est qu'ordre et beauté: tout brille. Comme on fait son lit, on se couche. Et je m'en voudrais bien de montrer autre chose que ce que je peux mettre en ordre, polir, orner, et ouvrir (car il fait beau *dehors*) aux rayons du sourire et de la volupté. (*S,* 70)
>
> [Here, all is but order and beauty: everything shines. He who makes his bed must lie in it. And I would resent myself for showing anything other than what I can put in order, polish, adorn, and open (because it is beautiful *outside*) to the rays of the smile and sensuous delights.]

Juxtaposing this passage with the famous Baudelairian refrain (1968, 112–13) whose elements it subversively adapts to its own materialistic reality, we once again agree to travel, not from here to there, but from there (Baudelaire's "là") to here (Ponge's "ici"), thus transforming the transcendental notion of an *ici-bas* (here below) into an *ici-haut* (here above), where, if properly prepared, one can be happy to live: "comme on fait son lit, on se couche" (he who makes his bed must lie in it). This preparation is the aim of Ponge's hygienic exercise. It is the iconoclastic refrain we read, the trip we take, on each page of his work. Guided by the poet's perspective, we rewrite Baudelaire: "*Ici* tout n'est qu'ordre et beauté, / Luxe, calme et volupté" [*Here* {replacing Baudelaire's *there*} all is but order and beauty, / Luxury, peacefulness and sensuousness]. As Ponge himself puts it:

> A tout désir d'évasion, opposer la contemplation et ses ressources. Inutile de partir: se transférer aux choses, qui vous comblent d'impressions nouvelles, vous proposent un million de qualités inédites. ("Introduction au galet," *Proêmes*, in *TP*, 198)
>
> [To every escapist desire, oppose contemplation and its possibilities. Useless to leave: shift one's attention to things, which fill you with new impressions, propose a million novel qualities to you.]

The trip is inside the wor(l)d—"un voyage dans l'épaisseur des choses" [a trip in the depth of things] (ibid., 199)—and uncovering the disregarded qualities of things is central to Ponge's notion of a curative poetry and to the poet's health: "[L]e plus important pour la santé du contemplateur est la *nomination*, au fur et à mesure, de toutes les qualités qu'il découvre...." [Most important for the health of the contemplator is the progressive *naming* of all the qualities that he discovers. . . .] (ibid.). This exercise will be hygienic, however, only insofar as it does not take one out of (linguistic) reality, as Ponge explains here, while playing on the literal and figurative

7 / Cleansing the Textures

meanings of the verb *transporter*, and sending us back to the Latin and Greek *metaphora*, transport, metaphor: "il ne faut pas que ces qualités, qui le TRANSPORTENT, le transportent plus loin que leur expression mesurée et exacte" [these qualities, which TRANSPORT him, must not transport him further than their deliberate and exact expression] (ibid.).

Ponge often relies on metaphor to relate the qualities of things, but his metaphors do not transport us by emotion, nor do they carry us out of the physical world. In fact, they underscore the material aspect of language. For example, according to the first poem of *Le Parti pris des choses*, "Pluie," even the cleansing rain, falling from the sky above, has the qualities of a coarsely woven thing: rain is "un filet . . . assez grossièrement tressé" [a thin thread . . . fairly roughly braided] (*TP*, 36). Caught in the net of rain is the common element of water itself, which is finely woven into the textual fabric. Ponge reinforces this subtler distinction by using the adjective "fin," which contrasts with "grossièrement," and signifiers containing *eau* (water): rain is also "un fin rid*eau* (ou rés*eau*)." On the one hand, this technique makes a distinction between coarser and finer textures of rain. On the other hand, it draws our attention not only to signified woven things as metaphors of rain but also to the various small pieces sewn into the poetic textures of words.

The analogy between the external world and the text as a woven thing is regenerated by Ponge's rain, itself a tissue, deriving from clouds that are tissues as well. The entire earth, in spring, erupts into one great complex of interweaving activity. A variety of smaller tissues is stitched together to compose the global tapestry of the natural world, as well as the variety of Ponge's poems where the same basic analogy is developed metaphorically:

Nous avons à redire *Novembre* comme on ouvre un tiroir (trop plein de perles et de vieilles écharpes), qui se renverse (et déverse son trop plein).

Mars est ici comme on secoue une dernière fois ces chiffons, comme on passe une dernière fois la serpillière.

Mais les broderies se reforment en vitesse — les canevas se remplissent à toute allure.

A partir de l'ancien canevas, les broderies qui sortent de terre, les fils qui sortent de terre et se nouent et (circulent) (progressent) (cheminent) se dévident et filent et se tissent, se tricotent,

forment franges, houppes, pompons, gansettes.

(*N*, 11)

[We have to repeat *November* as one opens a drawer (too full of pearls and old scarves), which turns upside down (and unloads its excess).

March is here as one shakes one last time the dust out of these rags, as one goes over the room one last time with the floorcloth.

But the embroideries re-form quickly—the needlework foundations fill up at full speed.

From the old needlework foundation, the embroideries that come out of the soil, the threads come out of the soil and join together and (spread) (progress) (advance) unwind themselves and spin and weave themselves, knit themselves together,

make fringes, tassels, pompoms, little braids.]

It is "*à partir de* l'ancien canevas" [*from* the old needlework foundation] that the weaving of nature is accomplished. A *canevas* (framework, basic structure) possesses the elements of a construction. The things that transcend the basic structure move beyond it while nevertheless remaining attached to it. They reuse the elements in their own way, by rearranging them or improvising on them. An analogical process can be observed in Ponge's text. The domestic metaphors of the passage gather together and play on the different meanings of a matrix word, *toilette*: a drawer full of finery and clothing such as "perles" [pearls] and "écharpes" [scarves], cleaning cloths such as "chiffons" [rags] and "serpillière" [floorcloth], and a series of little woven structures, reemphasized by the final diminutive ("les fils . . . forment franges, houppes, pompons, gansettes" [the threads . . . make fringes, tassels, pompoms, little braids]). In this way, the wovenness of the natural world is reflected analogically by human creations, a notion the poet has expressed elsewhere:

TRACES DE L'HOMME DANS CES GRANDS PAYSAGES EN RUINES MOUSSUES. — Traînées . . ., filons, cordelettes, chaînettes, *broderies minuscules* . . . : voilà tout ce que les hommes de par ici peuvent imposer durablement au paysage. ("Pochades en prose," in *GRM*, 87–88)

[TRACES OF MAN IN THESE GREAT LANDSCAPES OF MOSSY RUINS. — Tracks . . . , lines, small cords, small chains, *tiny embroideries* . . . : that is all that humans from around here can impose on the landscape on a long-term basis.]

Indeed, here human innovations are the work of the apprentices of the primordial spinner, the spider; its archetypal thread serves the arachnean Ponge as a *canevas* in the act of naming an aspect of modern communication networks that support the electric flight of weightless, coded discourse, and that appear, in this passage, as dew-adorned, suspended secretions:

7 / Cleansing the Textures 137

Il y a aussi ces fils de la vierge ces imperceptibles traînées de rubans des lignes télégraphiques avec leurs petits isoloirs de porcelaine qui brillent comme des gouttelettes. (Ibid., 88)

[There are also these gossamer threads {"fils de la vierge," i.e., threads that flutter about in the air . . . and that are produced by diverse spiders, according to Littré}, these imperceptible ribbonlike telegraph lines with their little porcelain insulators that shine like droplets.]

The analogy between human and natural creations arising from preexistent basic structures is reflected by the very words the poet invents and their sometimes idiosyncratic relationship to the languages from which French derived. For example, Ponge tells us that he built the first word of his title, *Nioque de l'Avant-Printemps*, phonetically, upon the analogical framework of the ancestral Greek language. However, the reader to whom the following passage is addressed must pay close attention to the first elements of language—letters and the sounds they represent. If they are neglected, the implication of the network rising above and transcending them, the text moving beyond them, may go unnoticed, for it will seem rather insignificant. At the very beginning of the text, Ponge declares:

NIOQUE est l'écriture phonétique (comme on pourrait écrire *inivrant*) de GNOQUE, mot forgé par moi à partir de la racine grecque signifiant *connaissance*. . . .

("Au lecteur," in *N*, 7)

[NIOQUE is the phonetic transcription (as one could write *inivrant*) of GNOQUE, a word I coined from the Greek root meaning *knowledge*. . . .]

We can appreciate the fact that Ponge coined the word, without, however, naively accepting that it is the phonetic transcription of the Greek elements upon which he says it is constructed. In fact, *Nioque* is phonetically incorrect for a word using the Greek *gnosis*, knowledge, as a point of departure. As we know, *gnosis* produces, in French, the word *gnose*, of which both the *g* and the *n* are *pronounced* [gnoz]. Likewise, any other word built upon this analogy would, theoretically, have to respect the phonetic autonomy of *g* and of *n*, as do all existing French words derived from the root *gnosis* (e.g., *gnoséologie, gnosie, gnosticisme*). But this is not the case with Ponge's neologism *Nioque*. Clearly, this is an intentional aberration: such a learned author—who not only studied both Greek and Latin, but whose work also constantly stresses the materiality of the signifier—would never have unintentionally committed an error of this kind. Overriding proof can be found in the cohesion of the text itself; for even within the native tongue, a similar "mistake" was made in the very same sentence: there is no word in the French language to which *inivrant* corresponds phonetically; and it definitely does not reproduce *enivrant* [ãnivrã]. In this text about knowledge, Ponge is pretending not to know in order to tell us something about his notion of knowledge. Such an analysis leads us to the effect of this passage, which is to slow the reading process down by means of seemingly incongruous linguistic mistakes, and thereby focus our attention on the questions: What is knowledge? What is its relationship with words? From what do our ideas arise? And the answer that it ever so subtly suggests is: They spring, as does the vegetal tapestry of the earth, from a *canevas*, from the basic structure or framework containing those material elements that comprise every compound (linguistic) organism—the alphabet:

> [C]e qu'on obtient en traitant le moyen d'expression, autrement dit le signifiant, pour ce qu'il est, c'est-à-dire une matière, matière à sensations, dont nous sommes en pouvoir de permuter les éléments, est en mesure de nous satisfaire supérieurement à ce que l'on prétend obtenir, mais on n'obtient *rien*, on n'*arrive* à rien, en *partant* (c'est le cas de le dire) (car, en effet, on en est parti pour n'y revenir jamais) d'un signifié antérieur: dit supérieur, ou transcendant. ("Braque, un méditatif à l'oeuvre," in *AC*, 312)

> [What is obtained by treating the means of expression, in other words the signifier, as what it is, that is, as matter, perceptible matter, whose elements it is within our power to permute, is in a position of satisfying us to a greater extent than what one claims to obtain, but one obtains *nothing*, one *arrives* at nothing, by *starting* (it is time to say it) (for, indeed, one has started off on the wrong track, never to return to the matter) with a preconceived signified: called superior, or transcendent.]

The permutation of these elements is to the tapestry of the mind what the arrangement of the chemical elements is to the woven world. The wor(l)d is woven "à partir de l'ancien canevas" (based on the old needlework foundation); and elemental deviation from the framework is precisely what produces a new entity in nature or in the mind: "Ce que je conçois comme tel: une oeuvre d'art. Ce qui modifie, fait varier, change-quelque-chose-à la langue" [The thing that I envisage as such: a work of art. That which modifies, causes variation, changes-something-within language] ("My Creative Method," in *GRM*, 13).

7 / Cleansing the Textures 139

The poet has expressed his efforts to rearrange the elements of language in a biographical—but also, perhaps, allegorical—mode, during his interviews with Philippe Sollers:

> Dans l'appartement où je vivais avec ma mère, j'avais arrangé une petite pièce qui était un ancien cabinet de toilette, où il n'y avait qu'une chaise et une table, une petite table. Cette pièce était sans fenêtre, je ne pouvais pas y tenir longtemps. J'étais là un peu comme un anarchiste travaillant en secret. Quelles étaient mes armes?
>
> Eh bien, au mur j'avais épinglé un alphabet en gros caractères; et sous la table, il y avait mon Littré. Je travaillais donc à préparer ma bombe, avec des lettres et avec des mots. (*EPS*, 71–72)

> [In the apartment where I lived with my mother, I had arranged a small room that used to be an old lavatory, in which there was nothing but a chair and a table, a small table. This room had no window, I couldn't hold out in there very long. In there I was a little like an anarchist working secretively. What were my weapons?
>
> Well, I had tacked an alphabet printed in large characters on the wall; and my Littré dictionary was under the table. So I worked at making my bomb, with letters and with words.]

Ponge's writing process takes place in that room of the lodging (of language) devoted to personal hygiene, the "cabinet de toilette" [lavatory]. It is the room in which the elements composing the quasi totality of our human body and of the body of poetry are the most conspicuous: water and the poet in the flesh; the letters of the alphabet and the body of their permutations, the etymological dictionary. The poet who emerges from this symbolic room is renewed, in that he has purged himself, through the application of water to his exterior, sullied tissues, thus regaining an interior, emotional regeneration, a sense of well-being. As the human body is cleansed by the element that, in the main, constitutes it (water), so the body of our language is purified by its constituents (letters). Water is employed to disintegrate impurities in the clothing of our skin; letters are used to annihilate the dirt that has collected in the language enveloping us.

The cleansing process is an attack, a bombardment: the bursting of the junctures of filth, their separation by means of a projection of elementary particles onto their (semantic) nuclei; an enraged eruption passing through the top of our body, our mind, yet having its origin in the deepest element of our being, in our deep-seated desire, and spurting out onto everything we contain within us. Ponge's text on the old-fashioned, stove-top laundry boiler makes this clear: "la lessiveuse" [laundry boiler] and the poet have the same motivation—they share the same anger—and operate according to the same hygienic principle:

> La lessiveuse est conçue de telle façon qu'emplie d'un tas de tissus ignobles l'émotion intérieure, la bouillante indignation qu'elle en ressent, canalisée vers la partie supérieure de son être retombe en pluie sur cet amas de tissus ignobles qui lui soulève le coeur — et cela quasi perpétuellement — et que cela aboutisse à une purification. ("La Lessiveuse," in *GRP*, 83)

> [The laundry boiler is devised so that when filled with a pile of ignominious cloths the emotion inside, the boiling indignation it feels, channeled toward the uppermost part of its being, rains down onto this heap of ignominious cloths that turns its stomach—and does so almost constantly—and so that the process results in a purification.]

As we not only contain language but are also contained within it, the hygienic release of tension accomplished by Ponge's bomb is a literary explosion within the enveloping system of language, which is viewed not only from the outside, from which angle it is convex *(bombé)*, but also from the inside, where it seems concave, womblike:

> Si douces sont aux paumes tes cloisons...
> Si douces sont tes parois où se sont
> Déposés de la soude et du savon en mousse...
> Si douce à l'oeil ta frimousse estompée,
> De fer battu et toute guillochée.....
> Tiède ou brûlante et toute soulevée
> Du geyser intérieur qui bruit par périodes
> Et se soulage au fond de ton être.....
> Et se soulage au fond de ton urne bouillante
> Par l'arrosage intense des tissus.....
>
> (Ibid., 82)

> [So smooth to the palms are your outer surfaces...
> So smooth are your inner walls where there are
> Sodium carbonate and soap lather deposits...
> So sweet to the eye your hazy little face,
> Of hammered iron all decorated with guilloche.....
> Warm or burning and all stirred up
> By the interior geyser that murmurs regularly

7 / Cleansing the Textures 141

> And finds relief at the bottom of your being.....
> And finds relief at the bottom of your boiling urn
> Through spraying the tissues intensely.....]

We secrete into the secret interior of language as we rub word-tissue against word-tissue, causing the discharge of the regenerative seed that, upon its bombardment of the egg, starts the miracle of new being. Just so, in the pre-spring season, the bombardment from clouds in the form of rain—itself a tissue—serves to bring about new being in the form of a vegetal tapestry that preserves yet transcends its parental framework. Like that of "la lessiveuse," the orgasm of clouds, as they "se soulagent" [find relief] is simultaneously the "arrosage" [spraying]—a link indicated by the rhyme on [aʒ]—of mother earth, of the "urne" [urn] containing the constituents of things that are extracted through decomposition, the incessantly recycled, immortal seeds that rain fertilizes:

> Les feuilles mortes de toutes essences macèrent dans la pluie. . . . [I]l faut attendre jusqu'au printemps l'effet d'une application de compresses sur une jambe de bois. . . .
> Voilà ce qui s'appelle un beau nettoyage, et qui ne respecte pas les conventions! Habillé comme nu, trempé jusqu'aux os.
> Aussi, lorsque les petits bourgeons recommencent à pointer, savent-ils ce qu'ils font et de quoi il retourne. . . . ("La Fin de l'automne," *Le Parti pris des choses*, in *TP*, 37–38)
>
> [Dead leaves of all kinds macerate in the rain. . . . One must wait until spring for the effect of compresses applied to a wooden leg. . . .
> That's what's called an excellent cleaning, and which has no respect for convention! Clothed or naked, soaked to the bone.
> Therefore, when the little buds start to peep out again, they know what they're doing and what it's all about. . . .]

The explosion of Ponge's bomb is also an orgasmic release of regenerative seeds, whose reparative function is to prepare a poetic spring. In a similar fashion, the laundry boiler, as the hygienic poetic principle, contains both male and female: an embedded, cylindrical waterspout through which the boiling liquid rises and gushes forth joyously, trickling down the surrounding walls, inundating and regenerating the tissues it bears:

> [La lessiveuse] éprouve une idée ou un sentiment de saleté diffuse des choses à l'intérieur d'elle-même, dont à force d'émotion, de bouillonne-

7 / Cleansing the Textures

> ments et d'efforts, elle parvint à avoir raison — à séparer des tissus: si bien que ceux-ci, rincés sous une catastrophe d'eau fraîche, vont paraître d'une blancheur extrême...
>
> Et voici qu'en effet le miracle s'est produit:
>
> Mille drapeaux blancs sont déployés tout à coup — qui attestent non d'une capitulation, mais d'une victoire — et ce ne sont peut-être pas seulement le signe de la propreté corporelle des habitants de l'endroit. ("La Lessiveuse," in *GRP*, 85)

[{The laundry boiler} experiences an idea or a feeling of diffuse dirtiness from the things inside it, over which by dint of emotion, of boilings and of efforts, it succeeds in holding sway—in separating the tissues: so that the latter, rinsed under a catastrophe of cool water, are going to come out extremely white...

And indeed the miracle has occurred:

A thousand white flags are suddenly unfurled—testifying not to a capitulation, but to a victory—and they are perhaps not only the sign of the bodily cleanliness of those who inhabit the place.]

And it is the way in which the laundry boiler acts on its "idea" that is so very hygienic (morally, practically) for us; just as, for nature, the (proposition) "rain," contained within the darkened texture of the docile cloud, when formed anew by the power of the poetic breath is the source of the ethical cleansing and refreshment of the wor(l)d, and therefore of the mind.

Once separated, the tissues can be recombined in such a way as to refresh us—as follows, for example, by creating a new kind of (intellectual) baptism, with the help of poetic lather:

> Il y faut ce noyau de brouillard azuré. Ce tourbillon de très fragiles sphères.
>
> Cette prestigieuse (prestidigiticieuse) mise en scène derrière laquelle disparaît la mémoire.
>
> La mémoire de toute saleté se dissout et certainement la plus mauvaise solution en cette matière, consiste à ce que votre idée fixe ou celle de vos parents vous mène en laisse à vous tremper, les bras en croix, dans quelque fade affluent de la Mer Morte.
>
> Peau neuve! Place nette! (*S*, 31)

[This nucleus of azure fog is necessary here. This swirling of very fragile spheres.

This prestigious (prestidigiticious) staging behind which memory disappears.

The memory of all dirtiness dissolves and certainly the worst solution in this situation consists in your one-track mind or that of your parents

7 / Cleansing the Textures 143

bringing you on a leash to soak yourself, crossing your arms, in some dull tributary of the Dead Sea.
New leaf! Clean sweep!]

It is the mind that is regenerated, for what was "fade" [dull] now possesses fresh meaning in a different intellectual context. This "fade affluent de la Mer Morte" [dull tributary of the Dead Sea], that is, the Jordan River, like everything at death, gives up its elemental remains, which, in turn, are recombined in a new composite body. The new baptism is based not on the unreflective submission to the *canevas* of tradition—"votre idée fixe ou celle de vos parents [qui] vous mène en laisse vous tremper" [your one-track mind or that of your parents {which} brings you on a leash to soak yourself]—but on the adaptation of its elements. As it was in the Jordan that the Word made flesh was baptized, that river being an element of Christ's immediate environment, so our bodily tissues are immersed in *a thing* of our quotidian surroundings: a washbowl, a thing with which we accomplish the virtuous cleansing process, an iconoclastic act. The river where Christ himself was baptized is reduced to its simplest analogue, a washbowl, and the mystical ritual of baptism, instead of being accompanied by the trappings of traditional religious symbolism, is performed in a makeshift lavatory: "Mieux vaut, crois-moi, dans la moindre cuvette . . ." [It is better, believe me, in the least washbowl . . .] (*S*, 46). The relationship between concrete thing and symbol is evoked by the material sounding of a word, *crois* (believe), which recalls the Christian symbolism of a thing, *la croix* (the cross), thereby suggesting a subversive baptismal power for the materialist poet. It is poets who give speech to things, to soap for example, and it is poets who have the greatest responsibility; for they show us where the different worlds are stitched together, at that point where our tissue, our skin, meets that of the exterior world, and the world of artistic languages.

Ultimately, the metaphor of weaving and sewing serves to link the plastic arts, music, and poetry together into a vast analogy. The different arts are interwoven in a grand texture, the analogue of the analogical fabric of nature itself:

Par ailleurs, un orchestre relativement restreint, comme celui que requiert la litho, une espèce d'orchestre de chambre, voilà qui devait convenir à Braque, dont le propre est de tailler directement . . . dans l'étoffe de la nature, puis de tout réassembler et recoudre par grands ou moins grands pans ou lés, selon un ordre grandiose mais jamais théâtral, tout intime. (*AC*, 242)[5]

[Furthermore, a relatively limited orchestra, like the one lithography requires, a kind of chamber orchestra, that is what was bound to suit Braque, whose distinctive feature is his cutting directly . . . out of the fabric of nature, then reassembling and sewing everything up again by large or less large pieces or widths, following a grandiose but never histrionic procedure, quite intimate.]

Indeed, this intertwining of the various arts known as *culture* (culture) is also *couture* (sewing), not only metaphorically but also etymologically:

Mais Manet a eu le mérite de défaire, lui premier, les *coutures* (jeu de mots intraduisible en anglais) de la vieille bâche goudronnée abritant le cirque ancien; le noir (les noirs), grâce à lui, ont été, enfin, élevés à la dignité de couleurs. Une très belle couleur. (*AC*, 308)

[But Manet had the merit of undoing, he first, the *coutures* {stitches} (play on words, untranslatable into English) of the old tarpaulin sheltering the ancient circus; black (different shades of black), thanks to him, were finally elevated to the dignity of colors. A very beautiful color.]

Discoveries and progressions in culture are, thus, the undoing and reassembly of preexistent se(a)m(e)s. It is the fusion of signifiers in the history of the French word that, as Ponge remarks, cannot be translated into English: in French, *couture* is an old form of *culture*; that is, "culture" has its origin in *couture:* "Culture, s.f. . . . . . ÉTYM. Berry, *couture*; picard, *couture*. . . . Dans l'ancien français, *couture* ou *culture* signifie une pièce de terre cultivée" [*Culture*. . . . Etym. Berry, *couture*; Picard, *couture*. . . . In Old French, *couture* or *culture* means a piece of cultivated land] (Littré). And the plurality of meanings attached to the fused signifier(s) *couture/culture* = c[o]u[l]ture is to be seen in Braque, that "Maître de Vie" [Master of Life] (*AC*, 247), whose essence is ("dont le propre est . . ."), on the one hand, "de tailler directement . . . dans *l'étoffe* de la nature, puis de tout réassembler et *recoudre*" [{his} cutting directly . . . out of the *fabric* of nature, then reassembling and *sewing* everything up again], yet whose activity is not only signified, as above, by *couture*, but also, as follows, by *culture* (cultivation):

Cette maison [de Braque] ne donne pas sur la mer. Loin de là. Mais sur la campagne; une vue de campagne assez largement étendue. . . . Ce que je veux seulement en dire concerne le jardin. . . . Braque, semble-t-il, arrangeant ce jardin, a très peu modifié la Nature. Pourtant, il est marqué de son goût. . . . Rien que d'infimes modifications [like his "sewing":

7 / Cleansing the Textures   145

"jamais théâtral, tout intime"], semble-t-il, mais, de toute évidence, Braque a médité ce paysage, et, sans tenir compte du tout d'effets de perspective, mais plutôt d'un effet d'étagement, il a conjugué le jardin et la campagne environnante. Voilà. J'en ai assez dit. (*AC*, 301)[6]

[This house {of Braque's} does not overlook the sea. Far from it. It overlooks the countryside; a rather sweeping view of the countryside. . . . Braque, it seems, while arranging this garden, *modified Nature very little*. However, it displays his taste. . . . Nothing but minuscule modifications {like his "sewing": "never histrionic, quite intimate"}, it seems, but, quite obviously, Braque meditated on this landscape, and, without considering effects of perspective at all, but rather an effect of terracing, he *conjugated* the garden and the surrounding countryside. There. I've said enough about it.] (Emphasis added)

In similar fashion, "il faut cultiver notre jardin" [we must cultivate our garden], thus recreating the superimposition ("l'étagement"), the union ("la conjugaison") that preexists in the wovenness of the wor(l)d: the reconciliation of mind and matter, of humans and nature, in a garden "[qui n'a r]ien, bien entendu, de ce qu'on appelle un jardin à la française" [that has nothing, of course, of what one calls a (formal) French garden] (*AC*, 301):

Et voici, par exemple, ce qui se trouve donné à lire dans [mon texte] *La Terre*: "Or, la vénération de la matière, quoi de plus digne de l'esprit? Tandis que l'esprit vénérant l'esprit, voit-on cela? On ne le voit que trop." Il me semble que cela n'est pas trop loin de la *ratio* dont nous parlait tout à l'heure Lucrèce, ni de ce que nous donne souvent à lire Braque dans le *Carnet* de ses pensées; mieux encore, dans ses peintures. (*AC*, 297)

[And here, for instance, is what one may read in my text *The Earth*: "Now, the veneration of matter, what is more worthy of the mind? Whereas the mind venerating the mind, did you ever hear the like? One hears it only too often." It seems to me that this is not too far from the *ratio* about which Lucretius was just speaking to us, nor from what one may often read in the *Notebook* of Braque's thoughts; better still, in his paintings.]

The greatest artists, then, are those whose existence harmonizes the most closely with the model of the Arachnean mode of being, and who therefore overthrow the Cartesian notion of "Je pense, donc je suis" [I think, therefore I am], replacing it, as does the spider, with "JE NE SOIS QUE PANSE DONC JE SUIS" [I AM BUT PAUNCH THEREFORE I AM]. In this way, they are true "Maîtres de Vie" [Masters of Life], and not just "maîtres à penser" (masters of thought):

Métier. . . .

Un des plus grands mérites de Braque est que sa méditation, *id est* son recueillement en sa complexion psycho-physiologique, l'amène à refuser, à récuser, à résoudre les antinomies de l'ancienne culture. "Penser n'est pas raisonner." L'une des antinomies résolues ["recousues"] par lui est celle jusqu'alors admise entre l'esprit et la matière. (L'esprit vainc la matière, disait-on). Entre la conception et l'éxecution. . . .

Méditatif. . . . A propos de ce mot, Littré ajoute que "celui qui médite est tourné sur lui-même; celui qui contemple est tourné vers le monde extérieur" (?)

Encore une antinomie résolue ["recousue"] par Braque. (*AC*, 314)

[*Craft {Loom}.* . . .

One of Braque's greatest merits is that his meditation, *id est* his contemplation within his psychophysiological constitution, causes him to refuse, to challenge, to resolve the antinomies of the former culture. {Referring to the text's previous etymological paronomasia on the word *couture/culture*, and the prior image of both Braque and Manet as sewers, we might not unjustifiably, instead of "resolve *(résoudre)* the antinomies of the former *culture*," rather read this: "sew up again *(recoudre)* the antinomies of the former sewing *(couture)*"; this is so especially since the paragraph concerns the noun *métier*, one meaning of which is "(the) loom."} "To think is not to reason." One of the antinomies resolved {sewn up again} by him is the one admitted until then between mind and matter. (Mind over matter, one used to say). Between conceiving and carrying out. . . .

Meditative. . . . Concerning this word, Littré adds that "he who meditates is turned toward himself; he who contemplates is turned toward the external world" (?)

Yet another antinomy resolved {sewn up again} by Braque.] (Emphasis added)

Conclusion

It is fitting to end this study with an analysis of the weaving analogy, for it is central to Lucretius's understanding of the atoms, Ponge's vision of the text, and their poetic interrelations. It epitomizes the correspondence between Ponge's notion of a poetic cosmogony and the Epicurean's world of external phenomena: the variety of things in the world results from rearrangements of the preexistent atoms into different compound bodies, just as the multiplicity of words results from the myriad possible permutations of the same alphabetical elements; and the interweaving of atoms in the composite body is analogous to poetic composition understood in relation to the primal semantic nuclei of words such as *text*, which are unraveled and rewoven in the mind of the reader.

Ponge's recurrent image of a complex tapestry perpetually arising from an eternal elemental framework is a variant of the fundamental atomistic analogy between nature and text. This analogy underpins his work, like the *canevas* or basic structure the poet's many metaphors also develop. Our analysis has concentrated on his development of the atomistic analogy because it best explains Ponge's effort to rewrite the text-world analogy, following the preexistent model in *De rerum natura*. The fact that numerous variants exist points to the "dissimilar similarity or similar dissimilarity" at the core of analogy itself (Anderson 1949, 6). It also reminds us that what is at stake here is not only resemblance, but also difference, which is an essential aspect of Ponge's poetics: "Il faut, à travers les analogies, saisir la qualité différentielle" [One must, through analogies, grasp the differential quality] ("My Creative Method," in *GRM*, 41–42).

Ponge's idiosyncratic extension of his Lucretian model further reveals a poetics of analogical metaphor, or analogy in semantic development, whose suggestions we may formulate as follows: this text is to literature as this object is to the world; or, by metaphorical variation, this text is to the world as this object is to literature; or, by another metaphorical permutation, this object is to literature as this text is to the world. Words and things, literature and the world, have changed sides, exchanged places, crossed paths. Whereas in Lucretius, the primary concern is the obscure atomic nature of things, which the characteristics of language and the text illustrate, Ponge inverts the proportion and focuses on the nature of language and the text, elucidating it by reference to atomistic theories. The order of analogical "theme" and "phore" has been transposed, and in this way the same basic analogy, transformed by Ponge, reveals not only the similarity but also the difference between Lucretius's work and his own, as well as between his texts and the "things" (or "pretexts") that are their subjects.

Ponge's readings of Plato, the Bible, and Rameau are anchored in the atomistic perspective, which explains his remotivation of his precursors' writings and defines the status that they have in the setting of his project. Two main categories are indicated by Ponge's interaction with the intertexts that this study has discussed. Ponge's rapport with the atomists (especially Lucretius, the poetic continuator of Epicurus) is closer in kind to his affinity with Rameau than to the connection to Plato or the Bible. As a materialist, Ponge disagrees with Plato's idealism and is equally opposed to biblical metaphysics; but he supports the views of Rameau and Lucretius, which, according to the poet, harmonize with his convictions because both are equally materialistic.

The character of Ponge's poetic transformations depends on the category into which the precursor's text falls. When the text is opposed to Ponge's perspective, he supplants it by inventing an alternative to what it proposes, such as his tree of poetry in response to Plato's chain of poetry, as discussed in chapter 1, or his scientific explanation of the ark of the covenant in reaction to the metaphysical interpretation of it in Exodus, as discussed in chapter 2. When the text basically concurs with the poet's views, he nevertheless remotivates its contents by rereading it in the framework of his own writings. For example, he shifts Rameau's harmonic theories onto his own valorization of semantic density and the etymological motivation of poetic language, as discussed in chapter 3; and he extends Lucretius's analogical explications of nature to his personal cosmogony of textual phenomena, as discussed in chapters 4 through 7.

The intertextual relations of the first three cases—Plato, the Bible, Rameau—lead to the connecting thread of the fourth circumstance: Lucretius and atomism. It is Ponge's reaction against idealistic and transcendental perspectives that causes him to develop a materialistic vision according to which body and soul, reason and intuition, form and content, might be reconciled in poetry. Therefore, whereas the poetry arising from his confrontations with Plato and the Bible transforms them while undermining or debunking them, the poetry springing from the dialogue with Rameau or Lucretius does not seek to overturn, but to cooperate.

Ponge's manner of collaborating with atomism is to retain basically intact certain fundamental and poetic analogies that Lucretius had put forward long before him, or that scientists have proposed more recently, while either implicitly or explicitly making them tenets in the new context of his own contemporary poetics. His renewal of the atomists always entails this type of transfer, by means of which traditional atomistic notions are at once defended and expanded in an individual and highly imaginative way, which is similar to what happens in the investigations of modern science.

This movement itself could serve as a definition of poetry, for it strikes a balance between what is exclusively communicative and what is purely recreational. Indeed, it is recreational in both French senses of the word: "recréation" (re-creation) and "récréation" (recreation) (Rigolot 1978, 266). Ponge is fond of the formal fusion produced by the portmanteau word, as it reveals a combined, analogical motivation of signifier and signified, thereby conveying a highly charged, even explosive, semantic content. It fuses distinct semantic nuclei, and the reader transforms this core into a less massive configuration, thus causing the release of poetic energy. In this way, Ponge's views concerning his new poetic rhetoric are related to the mechanism of atomic disintegration specific to a particular object and, by analogy, to the poem whose subject is an object of the external world or of the world of texts.

Ponge's allusions to Lucretius's poem add density to the semiotic reality of his writings, for they encourage the reader's movement back in time and through the layers of language. This process corresponds to his metapoetic notion of language's *épaisseur sémantique* (semantic density/ thickness/depth): as the words of Ponge's text refer to other words, so his text refers not only to its apparent subject (usually a thing of the external world), but also to a thing of the world of texts, that is, to *De rerum natura*. Lucretius's work explains the nature of things, and the intertextual link to *De rerum natura* explains the nature of "things" in Ponge's work, that is, his texts as things. Ponge's rewriting of the atomistic analogy therefore centers his poetic discourse on the text as sign, as it transposes the application of the analogy from an explanation of the external world to that of the textual world.

As in his encounters with Braque or Rameau, Ponge also invokes the analogy between poetry and other arts in order to develop this vision. For example, as the texture of a given musical composition derives from the "thinness" or "thickness" with which its "harmonic progressions . . . are packed with alterations" (Hindemith 1968, 111), Ponge's compositions display a texture resulting from the extent to which this famous "semantic density" is exploited. The degree to which it is developed reveals the specificity or *adéquation* (appropriateness) of the text-thing analogy. In other words, textual appropriateness is revealed by means of the relative degree of semantic density in the text, and the differential quality of both the pretext (that is, the object-subject of the text) and the text itself is discovered in their interwoven analogical relations. These mutually balancing undercurrents of analogy show that Ponge's poetic rhetoric is at once inter- and extralinguistic, in that it presupposes a singular, ontological privilege on the part of the texture of external phenomena that can be re-created within the epistemological text(ure) of artistic languages.

The use of analogy in Ponge's work reveals that "analogy is central in our philosophical knowledge of things.... This is so because there is an analogy in the existence of things, linking them all, even the most diverse, to one another" (Anderson 1949, 1). Analogy is typical of our thought processes, and it is in fact we who, through analogy, forge the links between disparate things. At a time when there is a potentially overwhelming and catastrophic sense of separation between the phenomenal and the subjective, it is important to absorb and apply this understanding of the nature of things as inseparable from human, imaginative participation.[1] In Ponge's work, we encounter a poetry that is likely to exert a considerable attraction on readers who, feeling an undesirable separation from the various phenomena of the external world, would agree with Braque's statement, that nowadays "on cesse de voir après 25 ans" (one ceases to see after twenty-five years of age). Such readers might regard the work of art as a possible path to their reintegration into the natural world, whose welfare depends on their participation as an element in it. This very participation might also be the way toward their own well-being.

Ponge's writings can be understood as an activity whose aim is to accomplish a balance between counterproductive antinomies; the gap between these antinomies must be spanned by the human element with its inherent capacity for both reason and intuition: "Son pathétique manège, longtemps commandé par la distinction arbitraire de l'âme et du corps, l'est maintenant par celle, non moins arbitraire, de la raison et des facultés intuitives" [Its {the human race's} pathetic ploy, controlled for a long time by the arbitrary distinction between soul and body, is now controlled by the no less arbitrary one between reason and intuitive powers] ("La Seine," in *TP*, 552). By remotivating words, expressions and various textual elements, carrying a historical complex of associations, Ponge's text becomes an epistemological metaphor alternating between a past seedbed and a virtual garden whose blossoming depends on the reader: "Je parle et tu m'entends, donc nous sommes" [I speak and you hear me, therefore we are]. Historically conditioned words, and, as in this quotation, highly charged syntactical units—Descartes's famous "Je pense donc je suis" [I think therefore I am]— are rediscovered by the archaeological movement through language. But when Ponge perceives the thought patterns built on them as being detrimental to our well-being, as in his confrontations with Plato and the Bible, he bursts them iconoclastically. In so doing, he produces a radically different concept, brought about by the reformation of their content, while leaving their basic physical structure recognizably but ironically intact. The syntactic "shell" is opened, and to its original content are added elements joining the subjectivity—"je" [I]—to that from which it was separated— the "tu" [you] and "nous" [we] of the quotation. A form that has somehow remained irreducible to its constituents throughout the centuries—the Cartesian formula is received by the mind in one swift movement—is reduced to them here: Ponge's deformation of the formula forces the reader to slow down and actually look at the elements one by one. Our attention is no longer drawn only to the unit as a whole, but also to its potential for metamorphosis. The same material units, when rearranged, produce distinct composite bodies. Nothing is created out of nothing, according to Epicurus, and this is the cornerstone of his cosmogony. In the same way, Ponge's re-creation is based on the rearrangement of the same basic material elements that have constituted previous thought-composites, be they his own or those of others.

This process necessarily involves the reader in a very personal way. The movement his work advocates can be accomplished only by the cooperative effort of individual readers acting according to their own interior force, or free will, and, on the ultimate level, by the entire community of readers, as they creatively combine together as elements in the compound body of poetry. The interior force of the atom is what, according to Epicurus, enables it to fight, to resist. The atom is the model of the autonomous individual. Different readings also have their own interior force. They may collide with one another, repel one another, or cohere with one another in such a way as to retain their individuality, while they nevertheless construct a whole from the sum of their parts. This reading process is analogous to a fundamental natural mechanism as postulated in Epicureanism, and it is present in the workings of language. In this way, the reader is understood as a primordial element of the textual world. The text comes into being through what we may call the *clinamen* of mind: the reader, leaving behind predetermined modes of thought, swerves into creative participation with a new and different set of possibilities. This leads to the ethical aspiration of the text—that is, to speak like Epicurus, what I would call a poetic ataraxia, a state of tranquil, godlike contentment.

In Ponge's writings, this notion is suggested by the concepts of the *objeu*, and the final goal of the *objoie* (see *EPS*, 189–90; "Le Soleil placé en abîme," in *GRP*, 156; *S*, 126–28). That the human emotion of joy ("joie") is, in this portmanteau word, integrally associated with the object ("objet," "ob-") is significant, for it reaffirms the interrelating of the physical and the emotional, brought to the fore by the imaginative activity of the poetic consciousness. Furthermore, the dichotomy of subject and object is here rejected, and an opposing concept is embodied in the corporeal merging that creates the word *objoie*. The objective and the subjective are seen as mutually interpenetrating.

Only an exceptional poet is capable of opening the worlds contained within the objects that have become a neglected part of our daily existence. This is exactly what Ponge does. His writings give each reader the possibility of a creative relation to the most seemingly banal objects. The human being may penetrate the heretofore exclusively material phenomena ordinarily regarded as separate from subjectivity, and, by means of the bridge of imagination, bring about the integrative contact resumed in Ponge's well-known formula: "PARTI PRIS DES CHOSES *égale* COMPTE TENU DES MOTS" [TAKING THE SIDE OF THINGS *equals* TAKING WORDS INTO ACCOUNT].

When Ponge speaks of his desire to take into account the entire content of the meanings of words-as-objects, he is, by implicit reference to the evolution of consciousness, evoking the possibility of cultural transfer. This possibility is activated by Ponge's personal process of *translatio studii*: he inscribes his work within a tradition concerned with the transferring of intellectual and artistic heritage from one age to another, as well as from one place to another. His writings provide a link with, and thereby continue, his predecessors' work. The bridge between past and present is often the Greek or Latin languages, the conservation of which allows for the connection to cultural origins and the valorization of the elements of civilization. But for Ponge, the progress of civilization is founded also in the deviation of cultural atoms that are rearranged in the new poetic phenomena of his work.

When Ponge writes in *Le Savon*, "Voici donc, cher lecteur, pour ta toilette intellectuelle (si tu es de mes amis, tu en sens parfois impérieusement le besoin), voici un petit morceau de *vrai* savon" [Here, therefore, dear reader, for your intellectual hygiene (if you are one of my friends, you sometimes feel in urgent need of it), here is a little piece of *real* soap] (30), he is not only underscoring his transformation of the sacrament of baptism but also the collaborative role of the reader in the creation of the text. Furthermore, given the connection made in his various works between the text and a woven object—especially one that requires periodic cleaning, such as the recurrent "robe (des choses)" [robe (of things)]—the kind of reader cooperation invoked here can be understood in terms of the specific activities involved in the production and maintenance of such an object, namely weaving and cleaning. By means of the cooperative intellectual weaving processes of writing and reading, the grand texture of language that clothes us is to be reborn pure, thus reciprocally cleansing our mind and preparing our well-being.

Words, then, are tissues within which we live; they are the textures constituting our clothing, our "robes," our "pretexts": they precede the texture of our intelligence, for they are composed of the simple impressions from which derive, and to which correspond, our ideas; they are also, in another sense, our "pretexts," in that they are the bordered and bordering robes between us and the world. They are the place where we touch the textures of the world and where the textures of the world touch the textures of our mind. Enveloping us, they are, as it were, the doubling of the precious tissue that is our skin:

> Nous avons à redire la "nature muette à rangs profonds qui nous entoure", nous reprend aux épaules, nous mantèle, coiffe et cravate. . . .
>   Cela, ces formes prises par la nature muette, . . . vit, se brode, continue. (*N*, 32–33)

> [We must once again tell of "mute nature with deep rows, which surrounds us," takes us by the shoulders again, cloaks us, provides us with hat and tie. . . .
>   That, these forms taken by mute nature, . . . lives, embroiders itself, continues.]

Being the place of the overlapping of the two grand systems, the precise functioning of the hinges—the semes, the pores—is of the utmost importance to our interior well-being and to that of the external world, of which we are elements:

> D'ailleurs la nature en France c'est encore vous-même: industrialisée, commercialisée; des jardins, des pâtis, des labours, des fabriques de bois. Pourtant, la liberté et le vent et les oiseaux y gambadent, y dansent à l'aise;
>   La liberté par tous les pores (robinets) en jaillit. (29)

[Furthermore, nature in France is still yourself: industrialized, commercialized; gardens, pastures, ploughed fields, lumber mills. However, liberty and the wind and the birds leap about, dance about freely;
Liberty through all the pores (faucets) gushes forth.]

For the very being of the world depends on our participatory function within it. And we can have no individual, differential quality without fulfilling this function. We have the choice of either being indifferent to this connection or of giving it close attention. When it goes unnoticed, however, dust and grime collect on it and it becomes sullied; the pores are blocked. Now, since all harmony between us and the world must necessarily pass through this place, if it is filthy, the passage will be closed; we suffocate. The living breath and light of the world cannot make its way in to us, and we are prevented from moving toward, from secreting into, the world. This separation, engendered by indifference, is an alarming, dangerous state of affairs; it is capable of leading to catastrophe, to the eventual destruction of nature as we know it and therefore to the ultimate unhappiness of the human race: to a place of no return. On the other hand, we may exercise our choice in another, opposing way. We may reject such apathy and decide to adopt a personal bias, a parti pris, in favor of these points of linkage, these se(a)m(e)s formed between the textures of wor(l)ds, maintaining them in a state of cleanliness in order to allow for their, and our, integrative functioning. In so doing, we would accept the salvation and paradise that Ponge's work proposes, and say with the poet: "Il suffit d'abaisser notre prétention à dominer la nature et d'élever notre prétention à en faire physiquement partie, pour que la réconciliation ait lieu" [Lowering our ambition to dominate nature and raising our ambition to be a physical part of it is enough to make the reconciliation occur].

Notes

Introduction

1. The dictionary referred to is Littré 1863–64. The author-date system used here and elsewhere in the text and notes is keyed to the bibliography.

2. Many have contributed significantly to the study of this aspect of Ponge's work. See, in particular, Riffaterre 1974, 278–9 and 1977, 66–84; a version of this article appears in Riffaterre 1979: "Surdétermination dans le poème en prose: Francis Ponge."

3. The title of Lucretius's poem is subject to slight variation, which is allowed by Latin syntax itself. Although Ponge and some critics to whom I refer call it *De natura rerum*, I call it *De rerum natura*, following the edition I use.

4. All translations from French into English are mine, unless otherwise indicated; this includes translations of the work of Ponge and of other authors who write in French. I have done the translations myself because although sometimes published translations do exist, I do not always agree with them, and because many of the texts I quote do not have a published translation.

5. Compare Greene 1970, 592. A French translation of this important article has appeared in the *Cahier de l'Herne* devoted to Ponge.

6. First published in *Poésie 44*, the essay also appeared in Sartre 1947, 226–70.

7. See Plank 1965, 303–4. For Robbe-Grillet's views on Ponge, see Robbe-Grillet 1963, 61–64.

8. Derrida's text developed out of his contribution to the colloquium on Ponge at Cerisy-la-Salle in 1975 and has been published as Bonnefis and Oster 1977. Versions of the text have also appeared in the journal *Digraphe*, no. 8 (May 1976), and in the *Cahier de l'Herne*, no. 51 (1986). Derrida 1988 is a slightly modified French version of the bilingual edition.

9. Here and throughout the text and notes, material enclosed in curly brackets consists of my interpolations or comments. With regard to quotations from Ponge's work, such interpolations or comments are often reserved for the English translations.

10. For an excellent analysis of this aspect of Lucretius's work, see Serres 1977, 172–78.

11. See "Tradition and the Individual Talent," in Eliot 1975): "[T]he historical sense compels a man to write not merely with his own generation in his bones, but with a feeling that the whole of the literature of Europe from Homer and within it the whole of the literature of his own country has a simultaneous existence and composes a simultaneous order.

This historical sense, which is a sense of the timeless as well as of the temporal and of the timeless and of the temporal together, is what makes a writer traditional. And it is at the same time what makes a writer most acutely conscious of his place in time, of his own contemporaneity" (38).

Chapter 1. Ponge and Plato

1. Bernard Veck's recent book responds in part to Beugnot's suggestion. His excellent study illuminates the various interrelations between Ponge's writings and the works of four modern precursors: Proust, Claudel, Valéry, and Rimbaud. At the same time, however, he maintains that "la conscience, chez Ponge, de l'inéluctabilité intertextuelle, relève sans doute de sa culture lucrétienne-épicurienne" [the awareness, in Ponge's work, of intertextual inescapability, probably comes from his Lucretian-Epicurean culture] (Veck 1993, 15).

2. On the notion of "dialogue" as it pertains to the poet's work, compare Veck 1993: "L'oeuvre pongienne est fondamentalement dialogique, dans la mesure même où elle répond aux sollicitations qui lui viennent des autres [auteurs], dont elle cherche à se différencier tout en les 'comprennant,' dans tous les sens du terme" [Ponge's work is fundamentally dialogical, to the very extent to which it responds to the solicitations coming to it from other {authors' works}, from which it tries to differentiate itself while at the same time understanding and incorporating them] (16).

3. This is not to say that Ponge was the first to write about "common" subjects; the sixteenth-century *blason*, for instance, includes "vulgar" anatomical poems such as "Le Pet" (The fart) and "Le Cul" (The backside), which, despite the topic, received critical attention.

4. For a helpful discussion of this dimension of Ponge's work, see Collot 1991, 224.

5. This preoccupation may be seen in other works by Ponge. Compare, for example, this passage from *Le Savon*: "Je suis en train d'écrire ces premières lignes. Je n'en suis pas plus loin que vous. Je ne suis pas *plus avancé* que vous. Nous allons *avancer*, nous *avançons* déjà, *ensemble*; vous écoutant, moi parlant; embarqués dans la même voiture, ou sur le même bateau" [I am in the process of writing these first lines. I am not farther along *in the matter* than you are. I am not *ahead* of you. We are going to *move forward*, we *are* already moving forward, *together*; you listening, I speaking; passengers in the same car, or on the same boat] (9–10).

6. Indeed, Ponge associates himself not only with Malherbe, but also with several other "artistes mesurés" [deliberate artists] for whom he has great esteem, including J. S. Bach, Jean-Philippe Rameau, Mallarmé, and, of course, Lucretius.

7. On the dichotomy Ponge establishes between "Poésie" and "Parole," "Verbe," *Logos*, see his *PM*, 76, 78, 180, 228.

Chapter 2. Ponge and the Bible

1. Ponge had won the award for that year.

2. The notion of poetry as a craft recalls important aspects of Valéry's poetics. And, indeed, there are several points of contact between Ponge's work and Valéry's. But Ponge differentiates his work from that of the dominant poet of the preceding generation, especially as concerns any implied link between poetry and magic: "Plutôt qu'une oeuvre devant s'intituler comme celle de Valéry: Charmes ou Poèmes, nous tentons une oeuvre dont le titre puisse être: Actes ou Textes" [Rather than a work, like Valéry's, having to be entitled:

Charms or Poems, we are attempting to create a work whose title might be: Acts or Texts] (*PM*, 204). Ponge's idiosyncratic and perhaps self-serving reading of Valéry constitutes a rebellion against the symbolic blurring of the boundaries between the world of language and the external world, which is implied by the tie to the utterance of spells as revealed by the etymology of Valéry's *Charmes* (Latin *carmina*, incantation). His contentious relationship with the extremely influential Valéry corresponds to the relationship between Malherbe and the Pléiade, especially since Ponge perceives Valéry as an institutionalized figure (see *PM*, 298).

3. Concerning Ponge's preference of diversity and its relation to his "rejection" of monotheism, as well as to his general worldview, compare Jean Pierrot's insightful comments: "[I]l s'agira pour Ponge de célébrer en toute occasion le multiple au détriment de l'un (de l'Un).... Cette volonté de substitution ... du multiple à l'un, gouverne, à n'en pas douter, toute la vision du monde de l'écrivain. Elle justifie ... , au niveau de sa physique, son ralliement complet à l'atomisme épicurien" [It is a matter, for Ponge, of celebrating, at every opportunity, the multiple to the detriment of the one (of the One).... This desire to substitute the multiple for the one governs, without a doubt, the author's entire worldview. It justifies ..., on the level of his physics, his total rallying to Epicurean atomism] (Pierrot 1993, 182–83).

4. See Sartre 1947, 226, 229. On the significance of naming as expressed by Ponge himself, see *NR*, 177.

5. This is the complete author's dossier from which the poem "La Figue (sèche)" was produced. The poem has been published in *Le Grand Recueil: Pièces (GRP)*.

Chapter 3. Ponge and Rameau

1. Critical work on the writings of Ponge has tended to overlook the connection to music. However, some very interesting and insightful remarks concerning Ponge and the role of music in his poetry have been made, especially by Jean-Marie Gleize and Bernard Veck. In Gleize and Veck 1984, for example, the role of music in the poet's diaristic, "open" work entitled *La Fabrique du pré* (The making of the meadow) is analyzed. They point out, for instance, that the poet's metatextual reflection—his thought concerning the literary formulation of *Le Pré*—is at moments concerned with establishing the rules of a kind of musical writing. This effort seems to be motivated in part by Ponge's intuitions concerning the interrelations between the subject of the text and the following intertexts: Rimbaud's phrase "le clavecin des prés" [the harpsichord of the meadow], from his *Illuminations*; and the harpsichord solo from J. S. Bach's Fifth Brandenburg Concerto, which the poet perceives as a music of "tigettes et fleurettes" [little stems and little flowers]—a music whose notes are as brief as the monosyllable *pré*. And in his recent monograph on Ponge, Michel Collot devotes several pages to Ponge's exploitation of assonance and alliteration—"le concert de vocables" [the concert of vocables {or meaningful sounds}] as Ponge calls it—and its relationship with the semantic aspect of the poet's language, that is, Ponge's effort to found a "r-é-s-o-n poétique," which is a poetics that reunites the demands of both resonance and reason, both *r-é-s-o-n* and *r-a-i-s-o-n* (1991, 176–80).

2. Rameau 1965, 49. I have modernized the French spelling. Rameau's quotations are from Zarlino 1966, pt. 3, chap. 58. Zarlino is the theorist whom Rameau quotes the most in the *Traité*. Commenting on this analogy, Rameau states that it is "une définition si claire et si juste de cette partie fondamentale de l'harmonie" [a very clear and very accurate definition of this fundamental aspect of harmony] (49).

3. See Ponge's remarks concerning the Littré dictionary in "My Creative Method," in *GRM*, 19, and "La Pratique de la Littérature," in *GRM*, 272.

4. See "Le Soleil placé en abîme," where Ponge explains his poetics of the *Objeu* by saying that the skillful manipulation of "l'épaisseur vertigineuse du langage" [the breathtaking depth of language] creates "ce fonctionnement qui seul peut rendre compte de la profondeur substantielle, de la variété et de la rigoureuse harmonie du monde" [this functioning which alone is capable of accounting for the substantial depth, the variety, and the rigorous harmony of the world] (*GRP*, 156).

5. The entire poem and a translation of it have been appended to this chapter.

6. For an idea of the extensive wordplay in this passage, see the following translation into English, which includes explanations in curly brackets, and the note following it.

7. As is often the case with Ponge's poetry, it is practically impossible to translate all the wordplay into another language. My explanations, provided in brackets, are not exhaustive, but they do give an idea of the intense semantic exploitation operating in the text. Other wordplay present in this passage, and developed in the poem, will be discussed subsequently in this chapter.

8. For another, insightful analysis of the poem, see Garampon 1952, 41–86.

9. This is a common aspect of poetry; indeed, Roman Jakobson has defined poetry in similar terms, without, however, referring analogically to music; see Jakobson 1963, 209–48. Compare Barthes 1964, 206–12, where poetry is on the contrary said to be nourished by the syntagmatic imagination.

10. For another reference to the Greek meaning of *music* in relation to Ponge's notion of "harmony," see "Entretien avec Breton et Reverdy," in *GRM*, 301.

11. On Ponge's notion of "adéquation," see "My Creative Method," in *GRM*, 31, and "La Pratique de la littérature," in *GRM*, 276–77.

12. Translations of *De rerum natura* quoted in the text and notes are by W. H. D. Rouse and are taken from Lucretius 1975.

13. For an excellent discussion of the way in which the Latin language informs Ponge's writings, especially as this aspect of his work pertains to some of Lucretius's ideas, see Veck 1986, 367–98.

Chapter 4. Ponge and Atomism

1. Concerning the relation between the Epicurean cosmogony and modern scientific opinions, recent commentators have insisted on their concurrence; for example, George Prescott Scott states that "the picture of life's events Lucretius gives us is exactly the same one most modern scientists describe" (1985, 39).

2. See, for instance, the passage of Epicurus's *Letter to Pythocles* in Epicurus 1926, 61–63, where he describes and explains the rising and setting of the heavenly bodies in several different ways. Compare *De rerum natura* 5.509–33.

3. For an explanation of this ethical dimension of his work, see Ponge's *Proêmes*, in *TP*, 218–26; to this passage, the following observation may be compared: "L'homme juge la nature absurde, ou mystérieuse, ou marâtre. Bon. Mais la nature n'existe que par l'homme. Qu'il ne s'en rende donc pas malade" [Man finds nature absurd, or mysterious, or cruel. Right. But nature exists only through man. So he shouldn't be sick with worry about it] (*TP*, 240).

4. Ponge has often expressed this view; see, for instance, Bonnefis and Oster 1977, 64.

5. See *De rerum natura* 3.3–6, where Lucretius explains that he is following in Epicurus's footsteps; see also 1.921–50 and 4.1–25 for his claims to originality in his treatment of Epicurus's doctrines.

6. See chapter 1 for a more detailed analysis of this analogy.

7. Compare Ponge's "La Seine," in *TP*, 548–51, where the same idea is expressed.

8. Other poets view letters in a similar way; but Ponge's connection to atomism places the phenomenon in a special light.

9. Camus's letter to Ponge, which is quoted in the text (*S*, 37–38), makes this clear.

10. See, for example, Bertrand Russell's vulgarization of the solar-system model of the atom in Russell 1923, 2.

Chapter 5. How the Text Rewrites its Atomic Structure

1. "Le Carnet du bois de pins" has appeared in the author's *Tome premier (TP)*. Page references are therefore made to the latter.

2. The *clinamen* and its relation to Ponge's work has been discussed in chapter 4. For Lucretius's explication of it, see *De rerum natura* 2.220–24 and 2.250–60.

3. The image of the complicated paths of the labyrinth in Ponge's work is not limited to a single installment; Gaston Bachelard finds it in Ponge's "Escargots": "Elle [la terre] les [les escargots] traverse. Ils la traversent" [It {the earth} goes through them {the snails}. They go across it] (the passage Bachelard quotes may be found in Ponge's *TP*, 57). He then remarks: "Si l'on médite un peu cette image, on voit qu'elle correspond à une sorte de labyrinthe redoublé. La terre 'dévorée' chemine à l'intérieur [des escargots] dans le même temps où [les escargots] cheminent dans la terre" [If one contemplates this image a little, one sees that it corresponds to a kind of intensified labyrinth. The "devoured" earth follows its course inside {the snails} at the same time that {the snails} follow their course across the earth] (Bachelard 1948, 245). This is equally true of the image of the labyrinth in the "Carnet," especially if we consider that part of the fabric of Ponge's forest maze is the ancient topos of the labyrinth, which, according to Virgil's *Aeneid*, is at once a woven place and the place of interwoven activity: "As of old in high Crete 'tis said the Labyrinth held a path woven with blind walls, and a bewildering work of craft with a thousand ways, where the tokens of the course were confused by the indiscoverable and irretraceable maze: even in such a course do the Trojan children entangle their steps, weaving in sport their flight and conflict. . . ." (1940, 1:484–85).

4. My sources for the discussion of carbon are the *Larousse du XXe siècle* (1931), especially the articles "Bois," "Carbone," "Molécule," "Radical," "Stéréochimie," "Tétraèdre" and "Triangulaire"; and the *Encyclopaedia Britannica* (thirteenth edition), especially the articles "Carbon" and "Valency." I have intentionally referred to popular sources that reflect the basic knowledge that had already been attained at the time of the composition of the "Carnet." Although he was not a scientist, Ponge was most probably familiar with such scientific rudiments. Indeed, in interviews meant to illuminate the relation between his background and his writings, the poet himself insisted that his scientific studies had played a significant role: "Il faut dire . . . qu'en dehors de ma formation, disons des humanités latines ou grecques, j'avais également une . . . formation secondaire dans le scientifique, puisque j'avais fait latin-sciences" [It must be said . . . that in addition to my education in, let's say, the Latin or Greek humanities, I also had a . . . secondary education in the sciences, since I had been a student in the Latin-sciences program] (*EPS*, 58). For a thorough study of carbon, see Pacault et al. 1965.

5. That Ponge considered and exploited this etymological meaning of *strophe* is corroborated by comparison with the piece titled "Strophe," *Proêmes*, in *TP*, 195, which has already been examined in chapter 4.

6. Lucretius 1975, 2–3, editor's note. For Venus's role at the beginning of Lucretius's poem, see 1.1–5 and 1.21–25.

7. *Larousse du XXe siècle*, 1931 ed., s.v. "Bois."

8. On the critical notion of "overdetermination," see Riffaterre 1983, chap. 1.

9. My transliteration based on Littré's Greek.

Chapter 6. Lucretius and the Analogy of Atomic Texture

1. Throughout this chapter, the transliterations of Greek words from literary passages quoted are mine.

2. On the relation between critic and rhapsode, compare Maurice Blanchot's observation: "Le critique est une sorte de rhapsode . . . ; rhapsode à qui l'on s'en remet, à peine l'oeuvre faite, pour distraire d'elle ce pouvoir de se répéter qu'elle tient de ses origines et qui, laissé en elle, risquerait de la défaire indéfiniment. . . ." [The critic is a kind of rhapsode . . . ; rhapsode to whom one leaves the task, as soon as the work has been finished, of abstracting from it this power of repeating itself which it gets from its origins and which, if left within it, might unravel it indefinitely. . . .] (1969, 572).

3. The Latin in parentheses is the last phrase of book 1 of Lucretius's *De rerum natura:* "so clearly will truths kindle light for truths" (1.1117).

4. For example, *Oxford Latin Dictionary* and *Harper's Latin Dictionary*. Furthermore, Ernout and Meillet note, in their article "lego": "De *lego* existent beaucoup de composés. . . . Les composés ont tantôt la forme *-ligo*, tantôt la forme *-lego*, sans que les raisons de la répartition apparaissent toujours" [Many compounds of *lego* exist. . . . Sometimes, the compounds take the form *-ligo*, sometimes the form *-lego*, but the reasons for the distribution are not always clear].

5. The same words can also mean "to wind up the thread (of life)," as in this phrase from the *Aeneid:* "extremaque Lauso Parcae fila legunt" [and the Fates gather up Lausus's last threads] (Virgil 1940, 2:226–27).

Chapter 7. Cleansing the Textures

1. This poem dates from 1919 and it is Ponge himself who says that it is "le premier texte, je veux dire le plus ancien de mon oeuvre publiée" [the first text, I mean the oldest of my published work] (*EPS*, 48–49).

2. Compare Steven Winspur's perceptive analysis of the ethical dimension of Ponge's poetic act: "Ponge propose aux gens qui sont tentés par l'idée du suicide une guérison par le travail poétique. 'C'est alors qu'enseigner l'art de *résister aux paroles* devient utile', écrit-il. . . ." [To people who are tempted by the idea of suicide, Ponge proposes a cure through poetic work. "It is then that teaching the art of *resisting words* becomes useful," he writes] (1993, 243).

3. The play on *éponge* reappears in *Le Parti pris des choses:* "Comme dans l'éponge il y a dans l'orange une aspiration à reprendre contenance après avoir subi l'épreuve de l'expression" [As within the sponge, so within the orange there is an aspiration to regain composure after having endured the trial of expression] (*TP*, 46). See Jacques Derrida's *Signéponge* for a thorough study of Ponge's "signature."

4. Ponge has expressed this notion elsewhere: "(Qu'est-ce que la langue? lit-on dans *Alcuin*. —C'est le fouet de l'air)" [(What is a language/tongue? one reads in *Alcuin*. —It's an airwhip)] (*Proêmes*, in *TP*, 211). See also "Pas et le saut," *Proêmes,* in *TP,* 134, where the exact same words appear.

5. Just so, the spider "file et tisse, *mais jamais ne brode*" [spins and weaves, *but never embroiders*] ("La Nouvelle Araignée," in *GRP*, 198; emphasis added).

6. Compare what Ponge says about *Le Savon*: "J'insiste sur le fait que mon *texte* lui-même ne devait s'en trouver en aucune manière modifié. Il s'agissait seulement de le mettre en scène" [I insist on the fact that my *text* itself was not to be modified in any way whatsoever. It was only a matter of staging it] (*S*, 39).

Conclusion

1. It is worth remembering that for post-Kantian epistemology, phenomenal equals subjective: *phainomeno* means "I appear."

Works Cited

Anderson, James F. 1949. *The Bond of Being: An Essay on Analogy and Existence.* London: B. Herder.
Aron, Thomas. 1980. *L'Objet du texte et le texte-objet.* Paris: Les Editeurs Français Réunis.
Bachelard, Gaston. 1948. *La Terre et les rêveries du repos.* Paris: José Corti.
Barthes, Roland. 1964. "L'Imagination du signe." In *Essais critiques.* Paris: Editions du Seuil.
———. 1973. *Le Plaisir du texte.* Paris: Editions du Seuil.
Baudelaire, Charles. 1968. *Les Fleurs du mal.* Paris: José Corti.
Beugnot, Bernard. 1990. *Poétique de Francis Ponge.* Paris: Presses Universitaires de France.
Blanchot, Maurice. 1969. *L'Entretien infini.* Paris: Gallimard.
Bloom, Harold. 1973. *The Anxiety of Influence.* New York: Oxford University Press.
Bonnefis, Philippe, and Pierre Oster, eds. 1977. *Colloque de Cerisy: Ponge, inventeur et classique.* Paris: Union Générale d'éditions.
Broglie, Louis de. 1937. *Matière et lumière.* Paris: Albin Michel.
Cassirer, Ernst. 1963. *The Individual and the Cosmos in Renaissance Philosophy.* Translated by Mario Domandi. New York: Barnes and Noble.
Collot, Michel. 1991. *Francis Ponge: Entre mots et choses.* Seyssel: Champ Vallon.
Derrida, Jacques. 1984. *Signéponge / Signsponge.* Translated by Richard Rand. New York: Columbia University Press.
———. 1988. *Signéponge.* Paris: Editions du Seuil.
Eliot, T.S. 1975. "Tradition and the Individual Talent." In *Selected Prose of T.S. Eliot,* edited by Frank Kermode, 37–44. London: Faber and Faber.
Epicurus. 1926. *Epicurus: The Extant Remains.* Translated by Cyril Bailey. Oxford: Oxford University Press.
Ernout, A., and A. Meillet. 1959. *Dictionnaire étymologique de la langue française: Histoire des mots.* Paris: Librairie C. Klincksieck.
Garampon, Georges. 1952. *F. P. ou la Résolution humaine.* Paris: Aubier.
Gavronsky, Serge. 1979. *The Power of Language.* Berkeley: University of California Press.
Gleize, Jean-Marie, ed. 1986. *Cahier de l'Herne: Francis Ponge,* no. 51. Paris: Editions de l'Herne.
Gleize, Jean-Marie, and Bernard Veck. 1984. *Francis Ponge: Actes ou textes.* Lille: Presses Universitaires de Lille.

Goethe. 1969. *Faust et le second Faust.* Translated by Gérard de Nerval. Paris: Editions Garnier Frères.

Greene, Robert W. 1970. "Francis Ponge, Metapoet." *Modern Language Notes* 85:572–92.

———. 1986. "Francis Ponge, métapoète." *Cahier de l'Herne: Francis Ponge.* Paris: Editions de l'Herne.

Hesiod. 1929. *The Homeric Hymns and Homerica.* Translated by Hugh G. Evelyn-White. Loeb Classical Library. London: William Heinemann.

Higgins, Ian. 1979. *Francis Ponge.* London: The Athlone Press.

Hindemith, Paul. 1968. *Traditional Harmony.* Vol. 1. Mainz: B. Schott's Söhne.

Horace. 1926. *Satires, Epistles, Ars Poetica.* Translated by H. Rushton Fairclough. Loeb Classical Library. London: William Heinemann.

Ivask, Ivar. 1974. "Notes toward a 'Francis Ponge in Norman.'" *Books Abroad* 48, no. 4 (autumn): 647–51.

Jakobson, Roman. 1963. *Essais de linguistique générale.* Paris: Editions de Minuit.

James, Henry. 1987. "The Art of Fiction." In *The Critical Muse: Selected Literary Criticism,* Edited by Roger Gard. New York: Penguin.

Littré, Emile. 1863–64. *Dictionnaire de la langue française.* 4 vols. Paris: Hachette.

Longinus. 1953. *On the Sublime.* Translated by W. Hamilton Fyfe. Loeb Classical Library. London: William Heinemann.

Lucretius. 1975. *De Rerum Natura.* Translated by W. H. D. Rouse. Edited by Martin Ferguson Smith. Loeb Classical Library. Cambridge: Harvard University Press.

Marx, Karl. 1967. "The Difference between the Democritean and Epicurean Philosophy of Nature." Translated by Norman D. Livergood. In *Activity in Marx's Philosophy*, edited by Norman D. Livergood. The Hague: Martinus Nijhoff.

Montaigne. 1978. *Les Essais de Michel de Montaigne.* Edited by Pierre Villey. 2 vols. Paris: Presses Universitaires de France.

Nizan, Paul. 1938. *Les Matérialistes de l'antiquité.* Paris: Editions Sociales Internationales.

Pacault, A. Adolphe, et al. 1965. *Les Carbones.* 2 vols. Groupe français d'études des carbones. Paris: Masson.

Paulhan, Jean, and Francis Ponge. 1986. *Correspondance.* Edited by Claire Boaretto. 2 vols. Paris: Gallimard.

Pierrot, Jean. 1993. *Francis Ponge.* Paris: José Corti.

Pindar. 1957. *The Odes of Pindar.* Translated by Sir John Sandys. Loeb Classical Library. London: William Heinemann.

Plank, David G. 1965. "*Le Grand Recueil:* Francis Ponge's Optimistic Materialism." *Modern Language Quarterly* 26:302–17.

Plato. 1937. *Timaeus.* In *Plato's Cosmology,* translated by Francis MacDonald Cornford. London: Kegan Paul, Trench, Trubner.

———. 1938. *Ion.* In *Plato,* translated by Lane Cooper. New York: Oxford University Press.

Ponge, Francis. 1961a. *Le Grand Recueil.* Vol. 1, *Lyres.* Paris: Gallimard.

———. 1961b. *Le Grand Recueil.* Vol. 2, *Méthodes.* Paris: Gallimard.

———. 1961c. *Le Grand Recueil.* Vol. 3, *Pièces.* Paris: Gallimard.

———. 1965a. *Pour un Malherbe*. Paris: Gallimard.

———. 1965b. *Tome premier*. Paris: Gallimard. (Works contained in this volume: *Douze petits écrits*; *Le Parti pris des choses*; *Proêmes*; *La Rage de l'expression*; *Le Peintre à l'étude*; *La Seine*.)

———. 1967a. *Le Savon*. Paris: Gallimard.

———. 1967b. *Nouveau Recueil*. Paris: Gallimard.

———. 1970. *Entretiens de Francis Ponge avec Philippe Sollers*. Paris: Gallimard/Editions du Seuil.

———. 1971. *La Fabrique du pré*. Genève: Albert Skira.

———. 1977a *L'Atelier contemporain*. Paris: Gallimard.

———. 1977b. *Comment une figue de paroles et pourquoi*. Paris: Flammarion.

———. 1983. *Nioque de l'avant-printemps*. Paris: Gallimard.

———. 1992a. *Nouveau Nouveau Recueil*. Vol. 1, *1923–1942*. Edited by Jean Thibaudeau. Paris: Gallimard, 1992.

———. 1992b. *Nouveau Nouveau Recueil*. Vol. 2, *1940–1975*. Edited by Jean Thibaudeau. Paris: Gallimard, 1992.

———. 1992c. *Nouveau Nouveau Recueil*. Vol. 3, *1967-1984*. Edited by Jean Thibaudeau. Paris: Gallimard, 1992.

Rameau, Jean-Philippe. 1965. *Traité de l'harmonie réduite à ses principes naturels*. 1722. Reprint, New York: Broude Brothers.

Richard, Jean-Pierre. 1964. *Onze études sur la poésie moderne*. Paris: Editions du Seuil.

Riffaterre, Michael. 1974. "The Poetic Functions of Intertextual Humor." *The Romanic Review* 65:278–93.

———. 1977. "Ponge tautologique, ou le fonctionnement du texte." In *Colloque de Cerisy: Ponge inventeur et classique,* edited by Philippe Bonnefis and Pierre Oster, 66–84. Paris: Union Générale d'éditions.

———. 1979. *La Production du texte*. Paris: Editions du Seuil.

———. 1983. *Sémiotique de la poésie*. Paris: Editions du Seuil.

Rigolot, François. 1978. "Le Poétique et l'analogique." *Poétique* 35:257–68.

Robbe-Grillet, Alain. 1963. *Pour un nouveau roman*. Paris: Editions de Minuit.

Ronsard, Pierre de. 1963. *Les Amours*. Edited by Henri Weber and Catherine Weber. Paris: Editions Garnier Frères.

Russell, Bertrand. 1923. *The A B C of Atoms*. New York: E. P. Dutton.

Sartre, Jean-Paul. 1947. "L'Homme et les choses." In vol. 1 of *Situations*. Paris: Gallimard.

Saussure, Ferdinand de. 1972. *Cours de linguistique générale*. Paris: Payot.

Scott, George Prescott. 1985. *Atoms of the Living Flame: An Odyssey into Ethics and the Physical Chemistry of Free Will*. Lanham, Md.: University Press of America.

Serres, Michel. 1977. *La Naissance de la physique dans le texte de Lucrèce*. Paris: Editions de Minuit.

Sollers, Philippe. 1963. *Francis Ponge*. Paris: Seghers.

Spada, Marcel. 1979. *Francis Ponge*. Paris: Seghers.

Veck, Bernard. 1986. "Francis Ponge ou du latin à l'oeuvre." In *Cahier de l'Herne: Francis Ponge,* edited by Jean-Marie Gleize, 367–98. Paris: Editions de l'Herne.

———. 1993. *Francis Ponge ou le refus de l'absolu littéraire*. Liège: Pierre Mardaga.

Virgil. 1940. *Aeneid*. Translated by H. Rushton Fairclough. 2 vols. Loeb Classical Library. London: William Heinemann.

Winspur, Steven. 1993. "La Poéthique de Ponge." *The French Review* 67:243–53.

Zarlino, Gioseffo. 1966. *Istitutioni harmoniche*. 1558. Reprint, Ridgewood, N.J.: Gregg Press.

Index

Aaron, 39. *See also* Bible
Adéquation. *See* Textual appropriateness
Alchemy, poetry as, 44, 99–100
Alphabet, epistemological role of, 138
Analogical formalism, 87
Analogy: between atoms and letters, 22–23, 62–63, 84–88, 93–95, 147; importance in poetry of, 19, 120–21, 150; metaphorical development of, 121, 135–36, 147–48; remotivation of atomistic, 87–89
Anarchist, poet as, 139–41
Anaxagoras, 87
Ancestry, Ponge's use of, 38, 48–49
"L'Anthracite ou le charbon par excellence," 100–102
Aphrodite, 100
Apology (Plato's), 27. *See also* Plato
Apostolic act, poetry as, 41–51. *See also* Bible; Malherbe; *Pour un Malherbe*
"L'Araignée," 55–59. *See also* Spider, poet as
Architecture, link between music and, 60–61
Ars poetica, 28, 52
Ataraxia, 20–21, 152. *See also* Ethics (Ponge's)
L'Atelier contemporain, 52
Atomism, 73–89. *See also* Analogy: between atoms and letters; Lucretius; Science, links between poetry and
Atomos, 77, 81–82

Bach, J. S., 52, 55, 156n. 6, 157n. 1

Bachelard, Gaston, 159n. 3
Baptism, poetry as, 45, 127, 142–43, 153. See also *Le Savon*
Barthes, Roland, 111, 158n. 9
Baudelaire, Charles, 36, 134
Beugnot, Bernard, 21, 26, 29, 156n. 1 (chap. 1)
Bible, 23, 37–51, 148, 151; format of, 37. *See also* Malherbe; *Pour un Malherbe*; *Le Savon*
Blanchot, Maurice, 160n. 2 (chap. 6)
Blason, 156n. 3
Bohr, Niels, 73, 82
Bomb, text as, 139–41, 149. *See also* Anarchist, poet as
Le Bourgeois Gentilhomme (Molière's), 125
Braque, Georges, 20–21, 52, 114–16, 144–46, 149–50. *See also* Painting, analogy between poetry and
Broglie, Louis de, 73, 81

Camus, Albert, 86
Carbon, analogy between text and, 96–102. *See also* "Le Carnet du bois de pins"
"Le Carnet du bois de pins," 91–107. *See also* Carbon, analogy between text and
Church (Roman Catholic), 38, 42–43. *See also* Bible; Protestantism; Reformation (the Protestant)
Claudel, Paul, 156n. 1 (chap. 1)
Clinamen, doctrine of, 73–74, 76–77, 79, 95, 112–13, 151. *See also* Atomism; Lucretius; Reader, role of

Index

Collaboration, poetry as, 29–36, 153. *See also* Reader, role of
Collot, Michel, 156n. 4
Commonplace, role in poetry of, 123, 125, 130, 133, 143, 152, 156n. 3. *See also* Poetry: things as subject of
Communion, 45. See also *Pour un Malherbe*
Conflation, poetic use of, 40–41, 56, 58–59. *See also* "L'Araignée"
Cosmogony, Ponge's poetics as, 16–17, 27, 63, 119, 147, 151
Craft, poetry as, 44, 132–33
Cross, symbol of, 143
Culture: relation to *couture* (sewing), 144–46; transfer of, 152

Danaids, 119
Decomposition, 84–85; of body and mind, 116–17; textual composition and, 90–107
Democritus, 74, 79
De rerum natura, 16–18, 20–21, 27, 41, 44, 78, 84, 88–89, 99, 106, 108–21, 147, 149, 155n. 3, 158nn. 2 and 12, 159nn. 2 and 5. *See also* Lucretius
Derrida, Jacques, 18–19, 21, 155n. 8, 160n. 3 (chap. 7)
Descartes, 29, 145, 151. *See also* Dualism, resolution of
Diacritical marks, significance of, 96–97
Diaristic work, text as, 91–92, 102
Dictionary, physical world of, 15–16, 55, 139
Differential quality *(qualité différentielle)*, poetics of, 147–48, 150
Dualism, resolution of, 145–46, 150–51. *See also* Descartes
Duchamp, Marcel, 24

Einstein, Albert, 73
Elements, arrangement of textual, 23, 86–89, 93–96, 136–39, 151. *See also* Analogy: between atoms and letters; Atomism
Eliot, T. S., 23, 155n. 11
Empedocles, 99–100

Enthusiasm (poetic), 28. *See also* Inspiration
Epaisseur sémantique. *See* Semantic density
Epicurus, 16, 18–22, 25, 27, 33, 41, 43–44, 50, 74–75, 77–79, 81, 83, 90, 106, 114–15, 119, 125, 148, 151–52, 158 n. 2, 159n. 5. *See also* Lucretius
Epistemology, 123, 137–38, 150
Error, poetic role of, 138
Les Essais (Montaigne's), 112
Ethics (Ponge's), 21, 25, 83, 89, 119–46, 152–54, 158n. 3 (chap. 4)
Etymology, role in poetry of, 23, 25, 41, 47, 55, 57–61, 78, 98–99, 102–6, 116–17, 119–20, 129, 131, 144, 146, 148
Eucharist, 42–43. *See also* Bible; "La Seine"
Euclid, 75
Existentialism, 24
Ex nihilo, doctrine of creation, 49, 77, 106
Exodus, 38–39. *See also* Bible

Fabric, text as, 122, 128–29
La Fabrique du pré, 157n. 1
Father of the Church, Malherbe as, 43–44
Faust (Goethe's), 110
Fautrier, Jean, 52
Fertilization, poetry as, 141
Formal imitation, 59
Formula, text as, 96–97, 101, 105
Fundamental bass, theory of, 53–55, 58. *See also* Rameau, Jean-Philippe
Futurism, 24

Garampon, Georges, 158n. 8
Gavronsky, Serge, 21
Genesis, 41. *See also* Bible
Genius, poet as, 30
Giacometti, Alberto, 52
Gleize, Jean-Marie, 157n. 1
God, 39, 42–44. *See also* Bible
Goethe, 110
Greek, analogical framework of, 137–38
Greene, Robert W., 155n. 5
Guez de Balzac, 45

Index

Harmony, 54–55, 157n. 2, 158n. 10. *See also* Melody; Music, analogy between poetry and; Rameau, Jean-Philippe
Heisenberg, Werner, 73
Hesiod, 111
Higgins, Ian, 20–21
Homer, 32–33, 111, 127–28
Homology, text as, 22–23, 25, 42–43, 50, 61–63, 77, 81–82, 84–107, 114–21, 151. *See also* Semantic density; Textual appropriateness
Horace, 111
Hygiene, poetry as, 45, 122–46, 152–54. *See also* Ethics (Ponge's); *Le Savon*; "Toilette," as metaphor of text; Words, dirtiness of

Iconoclasm, poetry as, 51, 134, 143, 151
Idealism, materialism versus, 26–36, 51, 73, 148
Indifference, attack on, 123
Indignation, poetry motivated by, 140
Inspiration, 17, 27, 35–36, 131
Intertextuality, 89, 130, 156n. 1 (chap. 1), 157n. 1
Isidore of Seville, 15

Jakobson, Roman, 158n. 9
James, Henry, 110
Jesus Christ, 38, 40–42, 44–49, 143. *See also* Bible

Kernel-word. See *Mot-noyau*

Labyrinth, image of, 159n. 3
Laërtes, 127–28
La Fontaine, Jean de, 102–3
Lamartine, Alphonse de, 28
Language: as clothing, 124, 139, 153; material aspect of, 47, 135; phonetic playfulness of, 61; relation of metaphor to, 135
Languages, mixing of different, 100–102
Last Supper, 41–42. *See also* Bible
"La Lessiveuse," 140–42. *See also* Ethics (Ponge's); Words, dirtiness of
Letters, meaning of individual, 85, 96

Letter to Pythocles (Epicurus's), 158n. 2
Linguistic materialism, 48–50, 61–63, 119. *See also* Analogy: between atoms and letters
Linguistic sign, elements of, 15–16, 149
Literary history, woven aspect of, 109
Littré (dictionary), 15, 55, 57–59, 103–4, 111, 130–32, 137, 139, 144, 146, 155n. 1. *See also* Dictionary, physical world of
Logos, 28, 36, 120, 156n. 7; analogical use of, 46–47
Longinus, 111
Loom, mind as, 110
Lucretius, 16–23, 25–27, 29, 33–34, 38, 41, 43–44, 50–51, 62, 74–78, 81, 83–90, 93, 102, 106–7, 108–22, 125, 145, 147–49, 156n. 6, 158n. 1, 159 nn. 3 and 5, 160n. 6. See also *De rerum natura*
Lyricism, 16–17, 133. *See also* Romanticism

Macrocosm, microcosm and, 113
Magic, poetry as, 44
Malherbe, 31, 33–34, 38, 43–46, 60, 81–83, 156n. 6
Mallarmé, Stéphane, 156n. 6
Manet, Edouard, 144, 146
Marinetti, Filippo Tommaso, 24
Mary, 40–41. *See also* Bible
Marx, Karl, 23–24
Materialism, 17–18, 20–21, 23–24. *See also* Idealism, materialism versus
Matrix word, play on, 136
Melody, 54–55. *See also* Harmony; Music, analogy between poetry and
Memmius, 41, 114
Metaphor(s): clouds as, 131–33, 135; interrelationships of, 31; loom as, 146; rain as, 78–79, 135, 141–42; sewing as, 146; sky as, 33–34, 135; weaving as, 23, 25, 55–59, 79, 105–21; wind as, 126, 131–33
Metaphysics, 20, 32–33, 73, 119, 148. *See also* Idealism, materialism versus
Metonymy, 102–3

Mind: relation to *simulacra*, 117–18; woven aspect of, 109–11. *See also Simulacrum*: painting as, text as
Molière, 125
Montaigne, 112
Moses, 38–39. *See also* Bible
Mot-noyau, 22, 90, 106
Muse, poet and, 30. *See also* Idealism, materialism versus
Music, analogy between poetry and, 52–63, 148. *See also* Rameau, Jean-Philippe
Musset, Alfred de, 28
Myth, use of, 99–100

Name, Ponge's transformation of his own, 48
Naming, creative act of, 47–48
Nerval, Gérard de, 110
Newton, Sir Isaac, 75
Neologism, 137
Nioque de l'Avant-Printemps, 137–38
Nominalism, 17
Nouveau roman, 17

Objectivity, subjectivity versus, 35–36, 152–52
L'Objeu, poetics of, 152, 158n. 4 (chap. 3)
L'Objoie, poetics of, 49, 152
Odysseus, 127–28
Odyssey (Homer's), 127–28
Onomastics, 129
Ontology, 34
Orgasm, poetry as, 141. *See also* "La Lessiveuse"
Originality, poet and, 31, 76–77
Oxymoron, 125

Painting, analogy between poetry and, 114–16. *See also Simulacrum*: painting as, text as
Pantheism, 36
Paradigmatic poetry, 55–63. *See also* Music, analogy between poetry and; Semantic density
"Paroles à propos des nus de Fautrier," 40–41

Le Parti pris des choses, 16–17, 26, 77–81, 135, 141, 160n. 3 (chap. 7)
Pasteur, Louis, 98
Paulhan, Jean, 20, 38, 86
Penelope, 127–28
Phenomenology, 17, 161n. 1
Phonology, use of, 137–38
Picasso, Pablo, 52
Pièces, 130–32
Pierrot, Jean, 157n. 3
Pindar, 111
Planck, Max, 73–74
Plato, 23, 26–37, 73, 148, 151. *See also* Idealism, materialism versus; Rhapsode; Socrates
Poetry: curative aspect of, 134; new rhetoric of, 63, 125, 149; notions of, 26–36; symbols of, 30–36; things as subject of, 26, 123–25, 148
Poiein, 59
Poincaré, Henri, 73, 82
Ponge, prior criticism on, 17–22
Pontius Pilate, 38, 47–49; analogy between Ponge and, 49
Portmanteau word, 149, 152
Pound, Ezra, 24
Pour un Malherbe, 28–35, 43–45, 52, 81–82
Precursors, Ponge's appropriation of, 20, 25, 59–63, 77, 90, 106–7, 111, 127–28, 134, 147–50, 152
Process, product versus, 36
Protestantism, 37. *See also* Malherbe; *Pour un Malherbe*; Reformation (the Protestant)
Proust, Marcel, 156n. 1 (chap. 1)
Pun: poetic use of, 39, 41, 55, 58–59, 104; role in poetry of, 25. *See also* Matrix word, play on
Pythagoras, 60

Qualité différentielle. See Differential quality

Rameau, Jean-Philippe, 23, 52–63, 73, 148–49, 156n. 6, 157n. 2. *See also* Music, analogy between poetry and

Reader, role of, 28–29, 34–35, 95, 121, 147, 151–54
Reading act, woven aspect of, 120
Reason, reunion of intuition and, 75, 88, 150–51
Reconciliation, poetry as, 29–36, 148, 154
Re-creation, poetry as recreation and, 149
Referentiality, 18
Reformation, poetry as, 132–34
Reformation (the Protestant), 37–38, 43–44. *See also* Malherbe; *Pour un Malherbe*
Regeneration, poetry as, 141–43
Rehabilitation, poetry as, 123
Repetition, technique of, 50–51, 91
Rhapsode, 29, 32, 160n. 2 (chap. 6). *See also* Plato
Richard, Jean-Pierre, 19–21
Riffaterre, Michael, 22, 90, 106, 155n. 2, 160n. 8
Rimbaud, Arthur, 156n. 1 (chap. 1), 157 n. 1
Robbe-Grillet, Alain, 17
Romanticism, 17, 30. *See also* Lyricism
Ronsard, 112–13
Russell, Bertrand, 159n. 10
Russolo, Luigi, 24

Sapientia, 21. *See also* Ethics (Ponge's)
Sartre, Jean-Paul, 17–19, 21, 74
Le Savon, 45–50, 85–87, 124–26, 152–53, 156n. 5, 161n. 6
Science, links between poetry and, 75–76, 80–83, 87, 96–102, 149. *See also* Atomism
Scott, George Prescott, 158n. 1
"La Seine," 41–43, 159n. 7. *See also* Eucharist
Semantic density (*épaisseur sémantique*), 18, 54–55, 59–63, 102–6, 109–21, 148–50. *See also* Homology, text as; Textual appropriateness
Serres, Michel, 155n. 10
Simulacrum: painting as, 114–16; text as, 114–18
"La Société du génie," 53–55. *See also* Rameau, Jean-Philippe
Socrates, 27, 29–32. *See also* Plato

Sollers, Philippe, 18, 21
Spada, Marcel, 20–21
Spider, poet as, 56–59, 127, 145. *See also* "L'Araignée"
Spiderweb, mind as, 110
Stanzas, structure of, 96–99. *See also* Carbon, analogy between text and; "Le Carnet du bois de pins"; Text: atomic structure of
Stravinsky, Igor, 52
Subversion, poetry as, 38–51, 143, 148–49
Surrealism, 24
Synecdoche, 102

Tautology, 129
Text: atomic structure of, 90–107; birth of, 99–100; buckled aspect of, 95; semantic notion of, 23, 56–59, 108–22, 147; woven aspect of, 153. *See also* Carbon, analogy between text and; "Le Carnet du bois de pins"
"Texte sur l'électricité," 38–40, 73–74, 82–83
Textual appropriateness (*adéquation*), 61–63, 88–90, 109–21, 150. *See also* Homology, text as; Semantic density
Textual harmony, 55–63. *See also* Rameau, Jean-Philippe
Thales, 74
Timaeus (Plato's), 32. *See also* Plato
"Toilette," as metaphor of text, 104–5, 126–30, 139
Tower of Babel, language as, 83
Traité de l'harmonie réduite à ses principes naturels (Rameau's), 53, 62, 157n. 2. *See also* Rameau
Transubstantiation, 42–43. *See also* Church (Roman Catholic)
Typography, poetic use of, 57

Valéry, Paul, 156n. 1 (chap. 1), 156–57n. 2 (chap. 2)
Veck, Bernard, 156nn. 1 and 2, 157n. 1, 158n. 13
Venus, 20, 99–100, 104–5, 160n. 6
Verse, Ponge's use of, 92–96. *See also* "Le Carnet du bois de pins"

Virgil, 159n. 3, 160n. 5 (chap. 6)
Vision: relation to *simulacra*, 117–18. *See also* Painting, analogy between poetry and; *Simulacrum*: painting as, text as

Weaving, analogy of atomic, 108–21
Winspur, Steven, 160n. 2 (chap. 7)
Words, dirtiness of, 124, 153–54. *See also* Ethics (Ponge's); Hygiene, poetry as; *Le Savon*; "Toilette," as metaphor of text
World: vision of word and, 89, 122, 142, 145, 154; woven aspect of, 118–19, 143–45, 153–54. *See also* Reconciliation, poetry as

Zarlino, Gioseffo, 53, 157n. 2. *See also* Rameau, Jean-Philippe